Pioneer
Free Will Baptist
Ministers
Burial Locations
In
Arkansas

This book was printed in the United States of America.

To order additional copies of this book, contact:
FWB Publications
Enchanting Acres
1006 Rayme Drive
Columbus, Ohio 43207
Alton.loveless@prodigy.net
Or
www.amazon.com

FWB
FWB Publications

Introduction

Arkansas

This book represents all that were part of the Free Will Baptist movement, consisting of the Palmer (south), Randall (north) and others such as the Stone, John-Thomas, John Wheeler Assns., NC OFWB and more.

Many of the photos are poor quality, but it was all I could find. Likewise, I do not have photos or tombstones for many of them. The information about these ministers were all that was available to me or found in archives. I made every effort to include those for which they would be remembered. Some I had no information, but research had shown they were of our denomination.

This Section is taken for a two Volume set done by this author.

PIONEER FREE WILL BAPTIST MINISTERS BURIAL LOCATIONS IN ARKANSAS

Arkansas

John O Adrian
Birth:
1850
Death:
1895
Burial:
Duty Cemetery
Lesterville
Randolph County, Arkansas

Early FWB preacher in the General Free Will Baptist Assn.

John Wesley Allred
BIRTH
13 Oct 1870
DEATH   4 Dec 1945 (aged 75)
BURIAL
Rogers Cemetery
Rogers, Benton County,
Arkansas, USA

Minister in the Old Mount Zion minutes in 1919.

Curtis H Ashcraft
BIRTH
26 Jan 1910
DEATH
10 Oct 1960 (aged 50)
BURIAL
Mulberry Cemetery
England, Lonoke County,
Arkansas,
PLOT   Section A

Rev Ozro A. Ashcraft
Birth:
Feb. 16, 1871
Arkansas
Death:

Feb. 18, 1946
Cleveland County
Arkansas
Burial:
Prosperity Cemetery
Pansy
Cleveland County
Arkansas, USA

Wed Sarah Elizabeth Patrick on 25 Jan 1894 in Cleveland, Arkansas and had 4 known children.

He was an early Free Will Baptist minister, in Arkansas, as shown in old church records and minutes, and in 1932 was living at Herbine, Arkansas.

Rev Robert Anderson Ashmore
BIRTH
19 May 1929
Pope County, Arkansas, USA
DEATH
4 Oct 1975 (aged 46)
BURIAL
Rest Haven Memorial Park
Russellville, Pope County,
Arkansas, USA

Rev. Robert Ashmore was an ordained Free Will Baptist minister and pastor, and in 1959. He was registered as a member of the Antioch Association of FWB.

Rev John Washington Atwell
Birth:
Dec. 21, 1895
Rudy
Crawford County, Arkansas
Death:
Apr. 13, 1986
Van Buren
Crawford County, Arkansas
Burial:
Mount McCurry Cemetery
Rudy
Crawford County, Arkansas,

A lifelong Crawford County resident, he was a minister and member of the 88 Freewill Baptist Church. Funeral services were held at Ocker Memorial Chapel, with Reverends Earl Gentry.

Elder Stephen Coonrod Austin
BIRTH
26 Feb 1855
Hardin County, Tennessee, USA
DEATH
10 Dec 1899 (aged 44)
Greene County, Arkansas, USA
BURIAL
Gainesville Cemetery
Gainesville, Greene County,
Arkansas, USA
MEMORIAL ID   60633494 ·
View Source

Stephen Coonrod Austin was the son of Henry Lamb and Mary Elizabeth Hardwick/Hartwick Austin. He married Rachel Caroline Sharp in Hardin County, Tennessee. Together they had eight children--Bartley, Henry, John, Zetta, Almeda, Stephen, Bertha and Ida Austin.

Stephen was an early-day minister in eastern Arkansas where he organized churches. He was a brother of Elder W. C. Austin, noted debater and preacher in Arkansas and Oklahoma. His name appears, along with his brother, in G. W. Million's book "A Brief History of the Liberal Baptist People in England & America 1606-1911."

Rev E Baldwin
Birth:
1860
Death:
1943
Burial:
Sandlin Cemetery
Ola
Yell County
Arkansas

Rev. E. Baldwin's name is in a roll of ministers for the AR State Association 1902, locally, The Western Arkansas Ass'n of the Free Will Baptists.

He is probably the "L.E. Baldwin," who mar. Mrs. M.L. Sanford, on March 2, 1898, Deisha Co. AR as shown in state marriages.

Rev Herman Dean Benson
Birth:
Jul. 22, 1930
Springdale
Washington County
Arkansas
Death:
Dec. 23, 1996
Washington County
Arkansas
Burial:
Shady Grove Cemetery
Springdale
Washington County
Arkansas

Lifetime resident of Northwest Ar. Freewill Baptist Minister. Husband Of. Ruby Benson
His name is listed as "Dean Benson" in AR State Association of Free Will Baptist ministers who had died from 1990-98. He was a member of the District Old Mt. Zion Association at time of his death, per report.

Rev Andrew Newton Best
BIRTH
13 Nov 1867
Nevada County, Arkansas, USA
DEATH
11 Apr 1942 (aged 74)
Logan County, Arkansas, USA
BURIAL
Landmark Cemetery
Chismville, Logan County,
Arkansas, USA

Rev. Andrew "A,N." Newton Best was the son of John Dolphin Best and Susan Catherine Tennessee (Benge) Best. He married Sarah "Sallie" Florence Woods on May 21, 1891 in Logan County, Arkansas.
He was an ordained Free Will Baptist minister in the Arkansas State Ass'n of Free Will Baptists in the early part of the 1900's, as his name is shown in old church records there.

J. W. Blanks
Birth:
Oct. 22, 1927
Flint, Genesee County, Michigan
Death:
Jan. 11, 2001,
Batesville,
Independence County,
Arkansas
Burial:
Egner Cemetery, Salado,
Independence County,
Arkansas

W. H. Bostic
Birth:
June 16, 1929
Rosebud, Arkansas
Death:
August 8, 2018
West Plains, Mo.
Burial:
Copperas Springs Cemetery
Guy, Arkansas.

He was a Free Will Baptist Minister for 54 years, of which he was pastor of the Allen Chapel Free Will Baptist Church for 28 years, where he was a member at his death. He was elected multiple terms on the State Executive Board which became the State Youth Board and was a strong instrument in moving the state of Arkansas into a state youth camp program. He has a son, Ron Blanks who is also a Free Will Baptist Minister in Missouri. He served as a medic in the United States Army.

"W.H. (Dub) Bostic, of Thayer, MO, was born the son of the late A.C. and Maybelle (Carter) Bostic in White County, Rose Bud, AR. He passed away at Ozarks Medical Center in West Plains, MO, at the age of 89.
Dub was united in marriage to Maxine M. Johnson on 1948 and were blessed to be together for 45 years. They had 2 children, David and Nelda. On November 20, 2002, Dub married Ina Smith Bennett.
Dub was a Free Will Baptist minister for over 50 years, pastoring churches in Arkansas, Texas, Missouri, Mississippi, and Oklahoma. He was also involved in Southern Gospel singing.

Rev Sterling E. Bowlin
Birth:
1938
Death:
1997
Burial:
Burkshed Cemetery
Washington County,
Arkansas

Shown in a List of deceased ministers in the AR Free Will Baptist State Association minutes, as being a member at time of death of the Old Mt. Zion Association.

Joe Burney Braddy
Birth:
Dec. 8, 1940,
Green Forest,
Carroll County, Arkansas
Death:
Jan. 20, 1993,
Fredericktown,
Madison County, Missouri
Burial:
Pickens Cemetery,
Green Forest,
Carroll County, Arkansas

He was killed in an auto accident and was pastor at First FWB Church in Fredericktown, Missouri at his passing.

Rev Thomas Brashear
Birth:
May 1, 1919
Pottsville
Pope County,
Arkansas
Death:
Jun. 30, 1985
Dardanelle
Yell County,
Arkansas,
Burial:
Saint Joe Cemetery
Atkins
Pope County,
Arkansas

Son of Thomas L and Amanda Suzanne (Braham) Brashear.

Ordained a Free Will Bapt minister and served last in the Antioch Dist. Association of FWB, AR. His name is documented in roll of ministers in the Minutes of the 1989 AR State Meeting.

Rev A Braughton
Birth:
Mar. 27, 1865
Death:
Jul. 22, 1938
Burial:
Union Cemetery
Johnson County
Arkansas

The Statistics On Death Have Not Changed. One Out Of One Person Dies

Henry P. Brown
Birth:
Oct. 16, 1926
Arkansas
Death:
Jun. 12, 2012
Springdale,
Washington County,
Arkansas
Burial:
Mount Hope Cemetery,
Vesta,
Franklin County,
Arkansas

Rev. Brown was a school teacher and a deacon before he became a preacher. Although a pastor himself, he did much to preserve history of ministers in making records and taping sermons and songs of other ministers.

He was a denominational leader and a World War II Army veteran.

James F. Brown
Birth:
Aug. 17, 1854
Henderson County
Tennessee
Death:
Mar. 17, 1922
Cleveland County
Arkansas
Burial:
Friendship Cemetery
Friendship,
Cleveland County,Arkansas

James Franklin Brown was born near Lexington in Henderson Co., Tennessee. His parents were Abner S. Brown and Emma Amie Reed. James F. was the last of the children to be born in TN. His Father moved the family to Arkansas around 1858 and homesteaded land in what is today NE Cleveland County Arkansas. At one time, James F. was a "circuit preacher" and traveled to various churches in the area to serve as Pastor for those churches. There are still a number of FWB preachers in the area who are of his descent.

Inscribed on stone
"I have fought a good fight, I have finished my course, I have kept the faith"

Harvey Benjamin Bugg
Birth:
Nov. 24, 1853
Johnson County
Arkansas
Death:
Jan. 13, 1937
Sebastian County
Arkansas
Burial:
Steep Hill Cemetery
Fort Smith
Sebastian County
Arkansas, USA
Plot: Southeast Section, Row 3

Harvey Benjamin Bugg was born to Benjamin Nicholas Bugg and Annis Tucker Bugg. His parents migrated from Tennessee to Arkansas in the 1840s.

March 1, 1860, Harvey's father was awarded a land grant for 40 acres in Johnson County. The document was issued from the Clarksville land office and signed by U.S. President James Buchannan.

According to the 1860 census, Benjamin, his wife, and children removed from Johnson County, to Sebastian County, Arkansas.

According to a contributor, old church records indicate H. B. Bugg, was an early Free Will Baptist minister as listed in the minutes of the Western Arkansas Association when it met in 1902. This Association included counties of Franklin, Logan, Scott and Sebastian.

J. H. Bullard
Birth:
Oct. 22, 1848
Tishomingo County,
Mississippi
Death:
Apr. 16, 1912
Burial:
Old Union Cemetery
Magazine
Logan County, Arkansas

He moved with his parents when he was four years old to Upshur Co., Texas remaining there till 1865 then moved to Hunt Co., Texas and in 1869 moved to Crittenden County, Arkansas where he married Louisa Manning. He was converted in September 1878 at Gilmore Station and joined the Methodists. In 1882 he united with the Missionary Baptist church at New Hope, in Mississippi County and was licensed to Preach. He was ordained August, 1886 and continued preaching till 1890 baptizing about fourty into the church. In 1890 he received a letter stating he was a consistent member and an ordained minister. With this letter he attended the Flat Creek Assn. of Free Will Baptists in Tennessee, which convened with the Union Church in Hardeman County in 1890 and was received as an ordained minister. He formed three churches—one at Wardell, one at Tyronza and another at Dead Timber, in Mississippi County, Ark.; and in 1892 formed the Tyronza Assn. He formed and assisted in forming thirteen churches and attended every session of the association being elect moderator in 1899. He baptized more than 300 persons.

Rev William Robert Burnett

Birth:
Mar. 3, 1857
Meade County, Kentucky
Death:
May 23, 1938
Hill Top
Boone County, Arkansas
Burial:
Hilltop Cemetery
Hill Top
Boone County, Arkansas

Rev. W.R. Burnett was an early pioneer Free Will Baptist minister in Arkansas. He was elected moderator of the 1918 session of the New Mt. Zion Association when it met at the Mountain View Church in Sept. 1918. Boone, Madison and Newton County churches were represented. When and where he was ordained, churches he pastored and other info of his ministry are unavailable.

Preacher William "Buck" Burnett; wife Sarah; sons: Alf, Jim and John. Hilltop about 1907.

George Washington Burris, Sr

Birth:
Jan. 18, 1856,
Atkins,
Pope County, Arkansas
Death:
Mar. 9, 1929,
Atkins,
Pope County, Arkansas
Burial:
Saint Joe Cemetery
Atkins,
Pope County,
Arkansas

From a October 4, 2007 newspaper article, noting the 120th anniversary of the establishment of St. Joe Freewill Baptist Church on October 7, 2007: *"In the year of 1885, George W. Burris organized a Sunday school under a bunchy top Gum Tree at St. Joe on Pea Ridge 10 miles north of Atkins. They had logs for seats and took School Readers to Sunday school. The Freewill Baptist Church was organized there in 1886."* .

George W. Burris was the principal leader there during his entire life.

Ordained Free Will Baptist minister, recorded in the Antioch Dist. Association of the AR State Association

Clarence Elijah Campbell
Birth:
Aug. 9, 1920,
Lost Corner,
Pope County, Arkansas
Death:
Aug. 10, 2011,
Hanford, Kings County,
California
Burial:
Rock Springs Cemetery, Hector,
Pope County, Arkansas
He was raised and educated in
Scotland and Greeley graduating
from Dover High School in 1942.
Clarence entered the U.S. Army
and served in Europe until his
discharge in 1945, earning the
Good Conduct Medal, EAME
Service Ribbon and Three
Bronze Service Stars. Following
his discharge, he obtained his AA
degree in business. Clarence was
ordained into the ministry in
Russellville and served as pastor
for Free Will Baptist Churches in
Arkansas, Oklahoma and North
Carolina for more than 30 years.

Rev Clyde Cleston Campbell
Birth:
Mar. 17, 1918
Hagarville
Johnson County, Arkansas
Death:
Mar. 14, 1985
Lamar

Johnson County, Arkansas
Burial:
Minnow Creek Cemetery
Hagarville
Johnson County, Arkansas

Third of seven children of
parents Grover Lee and Etta Sara
Jones Campbell. Married Vivian
Mae Smith. He was a Free Will
Baptist minister.

Glynn Campbell
Birth:
1925
Death:
Nov. 24, 2001,
Walnut Ridge,
Lawrence County,
Arkansas
Burial:
Lawrence Memorial Park,
Walnut Ridge,
Lawrence County,
Arkansas

Free Will Baptist minister who celebrated 50 years in the ministry. He pastored six churches in Arkansas and Missouri. He was an amateur ventriloquist. His son, Tim, became the Arkansas State Executive-Secretary.

Rev Willie R. Capps
Birth:
Sep. 18, 1906
Death:
Nov. 30, 1988
Burial:
Bland Cemetery
Rogers
Benton County
Arkansas

Rev. Willie R. Capps is listed in AR State Free Will Bapt. minutes roll of deceased ministers from 1980-89, from Old Mt. Zion Association. He was also in the previous list of ministers in 1958. When and where he was ordained and his pastorates, etc are not known. He was married to Clara O. Capps (1906 - 1978).

Rev James C. Carter
Birth:
1849
Death:
1921
Burial:
Lawrence Memorial Park
Walnut Ridge
Lawrence County, Arkansas
Plot: Section 8, Old Lane Block 6-7, Between Wren & Lark

He came from the Presbyterian Church and joined the General Free Will Baptists and ordained the year he joined. He was a quiet speaker and his favorite theme was the operation of the spirit. He did a great deal of good in this conference.

William Pleas Carter
Birth:
Apr. 14, 1854
Tennessee
Death:
Feb. 16, 1926
Warm Springs
Randolph County, Arkansas
Burial:
Carter Cemetery
Warm Springs
Randolph County, Arkansas

Early FWB preacher in the General Free Will Baptist Assn. who married Emily Jane Burrow Carter (1855 - 1938).

Enoch Thomas Chew
Birth:
Dec. 10, 1842
Indiana
Death:
Aug. 10, 1914
Burial:
Halbrook Cemetery
Conway County,
Arkansas

Enoch T. Chew married Sarah C. Upton 3 March 1870 in Perry County, Missouri.

E.T. Chew married Margaret S. Morris 27 June 1896 in Randolph County, Arkansas. Thomas Chew married Mary E. McKuin 10 February 1905 in Van Buren County, Arkansas. Son: James Zachariah Chew (1870 - 1940). Enoch died at 71 years of age.

Rev Earl L. Christian
Birth:
Nov. 2, 1916
Death:
Dec. 3, 1978
Burial:
Woody Memorial Cemetery
Rudy
Crawford County
Arkansas

Listed as an ordained Free Will Baptist minister in 1957 Minutes of the Zion Hope Association in western AR, when it met with Walnut Street FWB Church in Ft. Smith.
--from "History of Arkansas Free Will Baptists," by Rev. David A. Joslin, Editor, pub. 1998, pg. 14.

Inscription:
TEG5 US Army- World War II

Jimmy Lee Chronister
Birth:
Mar. 3, 1939
Russellville
Pope County, Arkansas
Death:
Jul. 22, 2014
Buttermilk
Pope County, Arkansas

Burial:
Walnut Grove Cemetery
Hector
Pope County, Arkansas

He was son of the late William and Syble Duvall Chronister.
He was a Free Will Baptist Minister and retired farmer, and member of the Sweet Home Free Will Baptist Church.
Jim started preaching January 1, 1965. He preached in the Antioch Association for one year before he was ordained as a Free Will Baptist Minister. He and his wife, Mary, pastored several churches in Arkansas, including St. Joe-Atkins, Union Grove-Atkins, Woodlawn-Russellville, First Free Will Baptist-Glenwood, Slaty Crossing-Dardanelle, Center Valley-Russellville (now Baker's Creek), Johnson-Scranton, Salem-Glenwood, Smith Springs-Morrilton, New Life-Morrilton, and finally Sweet Home Free Will Baptist Church of Atkins, where they have been since February 2004.

Rev Luther A. Clark
BIRTH
11 Jun 1892
Tennessee, USA
DEATH
10 Jul 1978 (aged 86)
BURIAL
Rose Hill Cemetery
Hope, Hempstead County, Arkansas, USA

Minister in the Zion Hope #2 Association of Arkansas Free Will Baptists, registering as such in meetings, (1959).

Arthur Edward Coffman
Birth:
Jul. 20, 1932,
Jerusalem,
Conway County,
Arkansas
Death:
Dec. 11, 2009,
Russellville,
Pope County, Arkansas
Burial:
Cedar Creek Cemetery,
Jerusalem,
Conway County, Arkansas

He was a member of the Dover Free Will Baptist Church. Bo was a Free Will Baptist Minister for 55 years (pastoring numerous churches over forty-nine years). He had numerous occupations over his lifetime: a farmer, a Dow Chemical employee, a MacDonald-Douglas Aircraft employee, owner and operator of the Coffman Tile Company.

Joseph Dempsey Coffman
Birth:
Jan. 11, 1892,
Hector,
Pope County, Arkansas
Death:
May 24, 1975,
Russellville,
Pope County, Arkansas
Burial:

Walnut Grove Cemetery, Hector, Pope County, Arkansas

Lawnie Coffman
Birth:
Feb. 22, 1922,
Arkansas
Death:
Jun. 3, 2008,
Arkansas
Burial:
White County Memorial
Gardens,
Searcy,
White County, Arkansas

Coffman received numerous awards and honors for his action with the 35th infantry during the World War II, including two bronze stars, two silver stars, four battle stars, and two Purple Hearts for being wounded in action. When asked about his heroic service, Lawnie once replied, "I did not mean to be a hero, I just did what had to be done. In 2004, Coffman was invited by public officials in France to return for a hero's welcome. During the trip, three different French towns honored him for his role in their liberation. After being struck in the shoulder by a large caliber 37mm shell intended for a tank during a battle in the Rual Valley of Germany, Coffman promised God that if He would spare His life, He would spend the rest of it doing the Lord's work. Lawnie kept his promise, pastoring for more than 45 years, and serving the Free Will Baptist denomination on the local, state, and national level. He is especially remembered for his role in establishing Camp Beaverfork, the state youth camp in Arkansas. In his book, *My Leg of the Race,* Coffman said, *"This I believe to be the greatest achievement of my church work."* He was one of Arkansas' most decorated soldiers.

Cecil Clement Cornett

BIRTH
3 Nov 1917
DEATH
8 Jul 1993 (aged 75)
BURIAL
Williams Cemetery
Warren, Bradley County,
Arkansas, USA

Orville C. "O. C." Cox
BIRTH
17 Feb 1911
DEATH
15 Aug 2007 (aged 96)
MILLSTADT, Ill.
BURIAL
Mount Zion Cemetery
Walcott, Greene County,
Arkansas, USA

He was born Feb. 17, 1911, the son of the late G.N. and Leva Eunice Howard Cox. He was a farmer and retired minister. He was the founder and former minister of the First Freewill Baptist Church in Paragould in the early 1950s. He was an ordained minister in the Baptist Association of First Freewill Baptist Church for almost 60 years.

Rev Oscar Lee Crabtree, Sr
BIRTH
11 Mar 1881
Crawford County, Arkansas, USA
DEATH
25 Feb 1968 (aged 86)
Van Buren, Crawford County,
Arkansas, USA
BURIAL
Gill Cemetery
Van Buren, Crawford County,
Arkansas, USA

Oscar Lee Crabtree Sr, 86 years old resident of Route 3, Van Buren, Arkansas, died Sunday, February 25, 1968 in a local hospital. A native of Crawford county, Mr. Crabtree was born March 11, 1881, the son of Isaac and Jane Morris Crabtree and was a retired minister of the Free Will Baptist church.

John Francis Crafton
Birth:
1836
Death:
Apr. 19, 1914
Burial:
Mount Carmel Cemetery
Sidney
Sharp County, Arkansas
Early minister in the Polk Bayou
Assn. Married to Malissa McKee
Crafton.

He was born to the late John
Emery Crossland and Lola
Hunter Crossland.
He was a pastor for 28 years for
the Faith Free Will Baptist
Church. He was a wonderful
husband, dad, Papa, Papa Jr. and
friend.

Emery J. Crossland
Birth:
Aug. 31, 1938
Tuckerman
Jackson County
Arkansas
Death:
Dec. 5, 2014
Hensley
Pulaski County
Arkansas
Burial:
Cheshier Cemetery
Elgin
Jackson County
Arkansas

John M Crouch
Birth:
Jan. 5, 1890
Death:
Apr. 30, 1987
Burial:
Forks of the Creek Cemetery,
Hector,
Pope County, Arkansas

He was a Free Will Baptist
Minister and pastored the
Kenwood church from 1952. He
was 93 in this photo.

Dec. 16, 1847
Tennessee
Death:
Mar. 28, 1920
Compton
Newton County
Arkansas
Burial:
Plumlee Cemetery
Compton
Newton County
Arkansas

Rev William Albert Crouch
BIRTH
15 Jan 1886
DEATH
24 Jun 1972 (aged 86)
BURIAL
Walnut Grove Cemetery
Hector, Pope County, Arkansas,

Ordained Free Will Baptist minister/pastor in AR, preached the intro message in the 1939 session which convened in Pike Co at New Hope church.

William was the son of James Calvin and Nancy Johnson Curnutt. He married Sabra Ann Reynolds on March 19, 1868. William Calvin was a Baptist minister.

He was an ordained Free Will Baptist minister, shown in old minutes in the 1918 State Association meeting at Mountain View Church. He listed his address as Compton, AR.

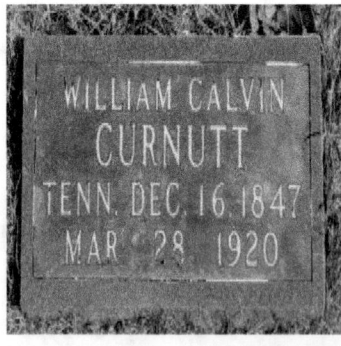

William Calvin Curnutt
Birth:

Rev Carl Davis
Birth:
Dec. 2, 1885
Death:
May 25, 1976

Burial:
Mountain Home Cemetery
Mountain Home
Baxter County
Arkansas

Rev. Carl Davis was an ordained Free Will Baptist minister, whose name appears in the 1960 minutes of the Big Springs Association, AR in a list of ministers, which Ass'n was organized in 1907, in north-central part of AR. He was listed as pastor of four churches. [i.e. one each Sun, which was a common practice in former years when there were not enough ministers for the churches].

Rev Eugene M. Davis
BIRTH
22 Nov 1911
Arkansas, USA
DEATH
3 Aug 1985 (aged 73)
BURIAL
Nelson Clay Cemetery
Clay County, Arkansas, USA

He was married to Clara Opal Cashion, 05 Aug 1944. He was in the military from 1942 (draft reg) for duration of war. Their son Thomas was born in Poplar Bluff, MO so they lived there for a time.

Eugene Davis' name is among minister's names enrolled from the Social Band Association of Free Will Baptists with other associations when they met in a state-wide session in 1958. After this time, they were not listed by name, and without an obituary, information is not known about his ministry, but his stone indicates he was a faithful minister until his death.

Thomas Sewell "Tommy" Day
Birth:
Sep. 16, 1910
Henryetta
Okmulgee County, Oklahoma
Death:
May 7, 1997
Springdale
Washington County, Arkansas
Burial:
Friendship Cemetery,
Springdale
Washington County, Arkansas

DAY spent 51 years in the ministry. He was the son of James Atlee Day (1888-1964) and Lula Lenorah (Nation) Day, (1889-1972). He was married to Mary Pearl (Shepherd) DAY for 61 years. She preceded him in death in 1993. Rev. Day was ordained as a Free Will Baptist preacher in January 1948. He was the founder of Phillips Chapel FWB Church in Springdale and pastored the church four years. He held membership there at the time of his death.

Bro. Day pastored 12 FWB churches in Arkansas, Oklahoma and Missouri during his half-century long ministry. He also did extensive evangelistic work in those states as well as in Kansas. Rev. Day served on the state executive boards in Arkansas and Missouri. He was active in the ministry even after he retired in 1975. He taught Sunday School until he was 84 years old.

Willard C. Day
Birth:
Aug. 25, 1913
Death:
Aug. 29, 1984
Burial:
Grace lawn Cemetery,
Van Buren,
Crawford County, Arkansas
He was the son of Francis Marion DAY (b. MO.) and Katherine (Catherine?) Mahalia (Hayes) DAY (b. AR.). He married Helen I. Chambers, May 1, 1934, in OK.
He was an ordained Free Will Baptist minister, who pastored in Oklahoma, Arkansas and Missouri. He was elected moderator and served the Oklahoma State Ass'n of Free Will Baptists in the 1950's. He was recognized as a teacher and taught from printed lessons on Biblical subjects he sent out to his radio listeners, and from which he taught in church schools. He was awarded a D.D. degree and was known among his brethren as Dr. Willard C. Day. He died of cancer problems in Ft. Smith, Arkansas. He became the first Promotional

Secretary in the state of Arkansas. He was also a member of the Foreign Missions Board in the early 50s.

Preston Clark "Press" Denton
Birth:
Jul. 9, 1883
Dublin
Logan County
Arkansas
Death:
Mar. 19, 1983

Clarksville
Johnson County, Arkansas
Burial:
Ware Chapel Cemetery
Cane Creek Township
Logan County, Arkansas

He was a member of Dublin Freewill Baptist Church and a retired blacksmith. His name is in a list of Free Will Baptist ministers in a book by Rev. David Joslin, "Hist of AR Free Will Baptists," showing ministers who had d. between 1980-89. He was shown as in the Antioch Association of Free Will Baptists. Date of his ordination is unknown.

Glenn G. Dipboye
Birth:
Jan. 9, 1903
Death:
Mar. 15, 1976
Burial:
Woody Memorial Cemetery,
Rudy,Crawford County,
Arkansas

Rev Larry Doggett
BIRTH
1 Mar 1947
Warren, Bradley County,
Arkansas, USA
DEATH
5 Jul 2014 (aged 67)
Monticello, Drew County,
Arkansas, USA
BURIAL
Pleasant Valley Cemetery
Warren, Bradley County,
Arkansas, USA

Pastor Larry Doggett age 67 of Monticello, AR died at the Drew County Medical Center. He was born a son of the late Rev. Oris Doggett and Ollie Sweeney Doggett.

Larry was the Pastor of Life Church, he was the morning DJ on KHBM radio station, president of the Drew County Ministerial Alliance, the Chaplin for the Drew County Detention facility and a bus driver for the Monticello School District.

Oris Doggett
Birth:
Nov. 27, 1918
Arkansas
Death:
Nov. 7, 1999
Burial:
Pleasant Valley Cemetery,
Warren,
Bradley County,
Arkansas

He married Ollie Sweeney, 18 aug. 1945, Bradley Co. AR. His parents: George W. and Sarah Margaret (Elder) Doggett.

He was a very active leader in the Arkansas Free Will Baptist movement serving Rev. Dogett served as pastor in various churches, and on the Ark. Exec. Board, in 1973, as well as other offices.

Rev Ralph E Doggett
Birth:
Oct. 22, 1916
Death:
Jul. 30, 1980
Burial:
Pleasant Valley Cemetery
Warren
Bradley County
Arkansas

Minister in Saline Assn.

Rev Henry Doyle
Birth:
Jul. 20, 1897
Death:
Jun. 11, 1984
Burial:
Ballews Chapel Cemetery
Grubbs
Jackson County, Arkansas

Husband of Gertie McCall Doyle.
Father of Ealem, Martha Elizabeth, William Harold, and Chester T. Doyle.

Henry Doyle's name was in the minister's 1958 Minutes of the AR State Association, and again in a list of deceased ministers from 1980-89, from David Joslin's book, Hist of AR Free Will Baptists. He reportedly d. as a member of the Polk Bayou Association.

Jefferson Davis "Judge" Doyle
Birth:
Sep. 21, 1861
Strawberry
Lawrence County,
Arkansas
Death:
Feb. 13, 1945
Walnut Ridge
Lawrence County,
Arkansas
Burial:
Lawrence Memorial Park
Walnut Ridge
Lawrence County,
Arkansas
Plot: Section 10 -
Old Lane Block 4-9

He was a early Arkansas FWB preacher and leader.

Adrian E Duvall
Birth:
1881
Death:
Sep. 9, 1937
Russellville
Pope County, Arkansas
Burial:
Hudson Cemetery
Moreland
Pope County, Arkansas

Funeral services were held this morning for Adrian E. Duvall, 56, Moreland, who died at his home Wednesday. The services were conducted by Rev. Dempsey Coffman. FWB Baptist pastor at Hector. Note: posted in Arkansas Democrat Sept 10, 1937.

Rev Ernest Hayden Elms
Birth:
Apr. 20, 1915
Independence County
Arkansas
Death:
Oct. 16, 1983
Burial:
Egner Cemetery
Salado
Independence County
Arkansas

A Free Will Baptist minister, shown in Rev. David Joslin's Hist. of AR FWB, in list of ministers having d. from 1980-89. He had served in the Polk Bayou Association of FWB at time of this report.

Rev Everett G Farnam
Birth:
Aug. 6, 1907
Death:
Dec. 31, 1989
Burial:
Hicks Cemetery
Lonoke
Lonoke County
Arkansas

Ordained Free Will Baptist minister in the Antioch Association in AR, shown in the 1958 State Minutes.

Rev Bennie Fisher
Birth:
Oct. 29, 1912
Death:
Oct. 30, 1994
Burial:
Mollie Gann Cemetery
Hatfield
Polk County
Arkansas

A ordained Free Will Baptist minister.

Rev Richard E. Ford, Sr
Birth:
Oct. 10, 1806
Warren County
Tennessee
Death:
Aug. 10, 1871
Benton County
Arkansas
Burial:
Blaylock Cemetery
Avoca
Benton County
Arkansas

Richard E. Ford was a Free-Will Baptist minister, who traveled from Tennessee to Arkansas and Missouri in a cart pulled by oxen. He had three sons, Josephus Wesley Ford, James Alexander Ford, and William Henry Ford who also became Free-Will Baptist ministers. Josephus and James went on to Texas and were active there and where buried. William is buried in Missouri. Each are in this book under those states. The 1850 census listed Richard E. as a wagon maker.

His Father Henry Ford, was b. 23 Dec 1767, Asheville, Buncombe, North Carolina; d. 11 Nov 1845, Cannon County, Tennessee (Age 77 years); Mother Mary Magdalene Moore, b. 8 Aug 1776, Asheville, Buncombe, North Carolina 28 Jun 1858, Maury County, Tennessee (Age 81 years)

He Married Martha Barham "Patsy" Middleton, b. 26 Oct 1810, Tennessee d. 5 Dec 1893, South Garfield, Benton, Arkansas (Age 83 years) Married 1826 Tennessee

Rev Charlie Glee Forrest
Birth:
Sep. 10, 1910
Death:
Apr. 30, 1995
Scott County, AR
Burial:
New Bethel Cemetery
Kingston
Yell County
Arkansas

Charlie Forrest, age 84, a resident of Plainview, AR died at Chambers Memorial Hospital hi Danville, AR. He was son to Foster and Floy E. Peeler Forrest. He was a cabinet maker and retired Free Will Baptist minister. He was a member of the Free Will Baptist Church.

Funeral services officiated by Rev. Scott Miller and assisted by Rev. Monroe Hunt.

Ralph J Fowler
Birth:
Jul. 27, 1922
Death:
Mar. 31, 1982
Burial:
Fowler Cemetery
Damascus
Van Buren County
Arkansas

His name is in a list of dec'd ministers of the New Hope Association of Free Will Bapt. in AR, from 1980-89. He was a veteran of
WW II Army

He began preaching in 1932. During his life, he helped organize 15 churches, preached more than 6,200 sermons, witnessed more than 2,000 professions of faith, baptized over 1,000 worshippers, conducted more than 1,200 weddings and about 2,600 funerals. His career included pastoring 12 churches, a radio ministry for 18 years with a broadcast every Sunday morning in his early years. Rev. Garrison was an evangelist with the Old Mount Zion Free Will Baptist Association for 19 years.

Cecil Oliver Garrison
Birth:
Oct. 2, 1909,
Pryor, Okla.
Death:
Nov. 6, 2003
Burial:
Bland Cemetery,
Rogers,
Benton County,
Arkansas

Rev Harold Hunter Garner
Birth:
Dec. 11, 1921
Death:
Jan. 14, 2002
Burial:
Rankin Cemetery
Lone Elm
Franklin County
Arkansas

Funeral services for Rev. Harold Hunter GARNER, 80, of Alma, Ark., were held at Mulberry First Free Will Baptist Church with Phillip Davis, Revs. Chester B. Smith and Cliff Ahart officiating. Pastor of Freedom FWB Church in 1997 Minutes

The Lord Is Coming

He was first a member of the Social Band Assn. but helped form the Union Band but later returns. He was one of the best students of the Bible and took a great interest in points of doctrine held by the FWB. He was clerk of the association and quarterly meeting a number of times. He married Minnie Lee Wright Gates (1882 - 1961).

Jesse Franklin Gates
Birth:
May 1, 1877
Arkansas
Death:
1962
Arkansas
Burial:
Masonic Cemetery
Pocahontas
Randolph County, Arkansas

Rev John Garvin
Birth: 1849
Arkansas
Death:
May 22, 1924
Washington County
Arkansas
Burial:
Burkshed Cemetery
Washington County
Arkansas

Rev. John Garvin, was the son of Samuel and Jane GARVIN. He became a minister, ordination unknown. He was listed as an ordained minister in the Old Mt. Zion Association of Free Will Baptists, in northwest AR, in its 1919 Minutes, the earliest available, being age 70 yrs, from Spring Valley (Washington Co). He was married to Martha Lyall, 12 Oct. 1873, AR. His parents were in 1850 Washington Co. census, and later, he and Martha lived in the Brush Creek township, Washington, Co., in 1900,

He was a retired drill press operator for Kay Chair Co. and a retired minister. He was a member and former pastor of 88 Freewill Baptist Church as well as several other area churches. He also was a member of Fine Springs Masonic Lodge.

Rev Earl W Gentry
Birth:
Mar. 24, 1914, USA
Death:
Nov. 21, 1994
Evansville
Washington County, Arkansas
Burial:
Mount McCurry Cemetery
Rudy
Crawford County, Arkansas

Dr John Campbell Gilliland
BIRTH
6 Oct 1932
DEATH
12 Mar 1988 (aged 55)
BURIAL
Rose Lawn Park Cemetery
Fort Smith, Sebastian County, Arkansas, USA

A minister, listed in roll from Old Mt. Zion Association of AR Free Will Baptists, showing he had died between 1980-89.

John David Glover
Birth:
Jan. 28, 1951
Star City, Arkansas
Death:
Jul. 10, 2014
Little Rock, Arkansas
Burial:
Kyler Cemetery
Batesville
Independence County, Arkansas

He was a retired meat market manager and a Free Will Baptist minister. He was a member of the Oakland Free Will Baptist Church at Bradford.

Kyle Elliot Goss
Birth:
Feb. 19, 1935
Pencil Bluff,
Montgomery County,Arkansas
Death:
May 28, 2012
Arkansas
Burial:
Woody Memorial Cemetery,
Rudy, Crawford County,
Arkansas,

He was a retired ordained minister, having served at the 88 Freewill Baptist and Catcher Freewill Baptist Churches.

Herman A. Greenwood
Birth:
Dec. 2, 1917
Death:
Mar. 22, 1999
Burial:
Pleasant Valley Cemetery,
Warren,
Bradley County, Arkansas

Popular minister in the Saline Assn. in southern Arkansas.

William M. Guinn
Birth:
Aug. 8, 1885
Death:
Sep., 1977
Burial:
Oak Hill Memorial Cemetery,
Booneville,
Logan County, Arkansas
Plot: Section 3-3; Block 25;
Row Ac.

Guinn married Mary Elizabeth Fritz in 1906 in Branch, Franklin County, Arkansas. Rev. Guinn was a Free Will Baptist minister and records reveal he was in Oklahoma in 1946 at the State Conference in Tulsa.

Don P. Guthrie
Birth:
Sep. 21, 1953,
Gassville,
Baxter County, Arkansas
Death:
Jan. 27, 1998,
Hot Springs,
Garland County,Arkansas
Burial:

Memorial Gardens Cemetery,
Hot Springs,
Garland County, Arkansas

A Free Will Baptist, church planter, and denominational officer. He was listed in *"Outstanding Young Men of America."* Pastored in Oklahoma, Texas and Arkansas. Chairman of the Christian Education Board of the Oklahoma State Association. Board of Trustees for Hillsdale College, Member of the Texas Home Missions Board and the National Home Missions Board. Chairman of the State Youth Board in Arkansas. He was a member of the Optimist Club and the U. S. Army National Guard. He graduated from Hillsdale Free Will Baptist College, Moore, Okla. and had a Master's degree from Southern Nazarene University in Bethany, Oklahoma.

Charles Wesley Hager
Birth:
Sep. 8, 1871
Arkansas
Death:
1944
Burial:
Whittaker Cemetery
Minturn
Lawrence County, Arkansas

Records conflict regarding the birthdate for Charles and his twin brother, Alfred. Some indicate they were born in 1871, others suggest 1872. Charles headstone lists the date as 1871 (Alfred's headstone says 1872). Minister in the Eureka church who attended the third annual meeting of the Union Band Assn. Spouse: Betty Vines Hager (1887 - 1937).

Rev Ed Hall
Birth:
Apr. 6, 1893
Death:
Apr. 20, 1964
Burial:
Thorn Cemetery
Greenbrier
Faulkner County
Arkansas

He served in WWI. He was minister in the New Hope Association in Central Arkansas.

Rev Faber Henry Hall
Birth:
Jun. 12, 1930
Death:
Aug. 18, 1996
Burial:

Thorn Cemetery
Greenbrier
Faulkner County
Arkansas

An ordained Free Will Baptist minister who ministered in AR. His name is listed in roll of ministers in the AR State Association roll of ministers, in 1959.
DS w/ Dwade E. Doyal Hall; married April 13, 1950; US Army-Korea; Back of Monument: children: Larry, Ronda, Eddie, Peggy, Faber, Jr.; Grandchildren: Hope, Charity, Elisha, Angel Rygel.

Rev Opie C Hargrave
Birth:
Aug. 1, 1920
Gassville
Baxter County
Arkansas
Death:
Jul. 31, 2010
North Little Rock
Pulaski County
Arkansas
Burial:
Conley Cemetery
Mountain Home
Baxter County Arkansas

Reverend Opie C. Hargrave, the day before his 90th birthday. He was born Gassville, Arkansas, the son of Grover Cleveland "Buck" and Myrtle Brewer Hargrave.
He served in the Air Force in World War II, and was married to Patricia Knight on June 5, 1948 in Tampa, Florida. He was a graduate of Columbia Bible College in Columbia, South Carolina, and served as pastor of a number of churches in North Central Arkansas.
Funeral services was held at Roller Funeral Home, with Bro. John Black and Reverend Mark Spripling officiating.
He served as Moderator of the Big Springs Association of Free Will Baptists in the 1960 session. His address was Mountain Home, AR. Unknown when and were he was ordained, as that is the oldest available minute for that association, which was organized in 1907.

Rev Velon Eugene Harmon
Birth:
Feb. 11, 1925
Boldman
Pike County, Kentucky
Death:
Jun. 11, 2014
Taylor
Wayne County, Michigan
Burial:
Cleburne County Memorial Gardens
Heber Springs
Cleburne County, Arkansas

He was born in Boldman, Kentucky to the late John C. and Gracie Keathley Harmon. He was a US Army Veteran of WWII and a Free Will Baptist minister.

Funeral service was at the Olmstead Chapel with Rev. David Copeland officiating. Interment was with Military Honors.

Rev Hosea G Harrelson
Birth:
Feb. 1, 1909
Death:
Nov. 30, 1989
Burial:
Bluff Cemetery
Springdale
Washington County
Arkansas

Ordained minister in the Free Will Baptist church, and a member of the Old Mt. Zion Association at the time of his death

Inscription:
DAD
THE LORD IS MY SHEPHERD
Plot: Addition:1979;
Section:12 A; Plot:3

Rev James Harrington
Birth:
Oct. 6, 1864
Missouri
Death:
Jun. 4, 1923
Carroll County, Arkansas
Burial:
Shady Grove Cemetery
Osage
Carroll County, Arkansas

Rev. Harrington was an ordained Free Will Baptist minister and a member of the AR FWB State Association of churches in 1918, when it met with the Mountain View church.

His name was in the roll of ministers, and his address was Osage, AR. When and where he was ordained is unavailable at this time. The 1920 census shows that he said he was born in Missouri. --taken from *"History of Arkansas Free Will Baptists,"* Rev. David A. Joslin, Editor, pub. 199 [pg. 34].

Rev Joseph Levi Harris
BIRTH
Aug 1863
Atkins, Pope County, Arkansas, USA
DEATH
12 Feb 1945 (aged 81)
Lepanto, Poinsett County, Arkansas, USA
BURIAL
Saint Joe Cemetery
Atkins, Pope County, Arkansas,

Former Pastor of St. Joe Free Will Baptist Church of Atkins The Rev. Joseph Levi Harris
He was in attendance in the 1941 Session of the AR State Association of Free Will Baptists and gave a short talk as 'one of the ministers over 50.'

Mark Metcher Harris
Birth:
Aug. 8, 1861,
England
Death:
Oct. 12, 1935,
Coaldale,
Scott County, Arkansas
Burial:
Coaldale Cemetery, Coaldale,
Scott County, Arkansas

Harris was born in England and came to this country. He was found in the Chickasaw Nation, I.T. before statehood, and was affiliated with the Free Will Baptist. In 1901, the Center Ass'n approved him for license, and in 1902 he was ordained. He served as clerk of that conference for about two years, when he was elected to be moderator. He pastored churches in the association until about 1906 when he and some of his family moved to Scott Co. AR., where he lived until his death, remaining faithful.

John R. Hartley
Birth:
1863
Death:
1942
Burial:
Shady Grove Cemetery,
Glendale, Lincoln County,
Arkansas

Rev Henry W Hart
Birth:
Aug. 30, 1924
Death:
Jun. 19, 1991
Burial:
Greene County Memorial
Gardens Cemetery
Paragould
Greene County
Arkansas

Born in Knobel, AR. He was an ordained minister in the Free Will Baptist church, listed in a roll of deceased ministers in the Arkansas State FWB Association in 1998 as being in the Social Band (District Ass'n) at the time of his death.

He was Jim Puckett's great grandfather. He married Barbara Ellen Anderson, who was born in 1867 and died in 1931. He pastored in Arkansas all his life.. His daughter – Lillian Geneva Hartley –married James H. McClellan. She was a devout Christian woman who died following the birth of her eighth child. Her eldest was just a teenage boy, and Jim's mother Anna, was the oldest daughter. At age 11, Anna remembers her father gathering the children around her mother's bedside just before she died. She told them all that she loved them and wanted them to live for the Lord and meet her in Heaven. From that day forward, Anna cooked, cleaned, sewed and raised her siblings. The entire family lived for the Lord, and their family heritage of godliness continued.

Anna's brother Elbert McClellan was also a pastor. Hartley pastored Macedonia Free Will Baptist Church from 1912-1914, and again from 1919 – 1925. Anna was born in 1919, during the time of his tenure. Rev. Hartley also had a son named Johnny who was a preacher. He never married. He did not pastor but did preach. He adopted and raised a mentally retarded boy name Nonie, and took care of him his entire life.

John S. Hartley
BIRTH
28 Dec 1897
DEATH
12 Nov 1991 (aged 93)
BURIAL
Shady Grove Cemetery
Glendale, Lincoln County,
Arkansas

He preached although did not pastor, but he was listed in the roll of ministers of the Saline Association of AR Free Will Baptists, in 1958. His father was a minister, and several of his descendants, including Rev. Jim Puckett.

Rev George W. Hassell
Birth:
1851
Death:
1921
Burial:
Barren Fork Cemetery
Mount Pleasant
Izard County, Arkansas

Rev. George W. Hassell was an ordained minister in the Polk Bayou Association of Free Will Baptists, when it met with the AR State Ass'n of FWB in 1902. When or where he was ordained is unknown at this time.
--taken from "History of Arkansas Free Will Baptists," by Rev. David A Joslin, Editor, pub. 1998, pg. 58

Rev George Julian Hawkins
BIRTH
19 Oct 1911
Alma, Crawford County,
Arkansas
DEATH
15 Feb 2004 (aged 92)
Van Buren, Crawford County,
Arkansas
BURIAL
Gracelawn Cemetery
Van Buren, Crawford County,
Arkansas

Freewill Baptist Minister. The date on his headstone (Oct 9) is incorrect. The date is October 19, 1911. Published Funeral Records Of Crawford County Arkansas Book of Burials Volumes One and Two in 1995 and 1996.

Honored here for his work in the ministry, especially Arkansas as pastor and leader. He served on Exec. Board of AR FWB in 1963 in organization of Unity Association, and in other capacities during his long and fruitful life.

Claude Joseph Hendrix
Birth:
1921
Death:
1996
Burial:
Benton County Memorial Park
Rogers
Benton County
Arkansas

His name is included in a list of deceased ministers in the Arkansas State Association of Free Will Baptists, his affiliation at the time was the Old Mt. Zion District Ass'n

Carl Leo High
Birth:
Jul. 10, 1913
Death:
May 6, 1983,
Arkansas
Burial:
Pirtle Cemetery,
Peach Orchard,
Clay County, Arkansas

He served many years as a leader and pastor in the Social Band Association in Northeast Arkansas.

Rev Edward Washington Hill
Birth:
Jan. 19, 1880
Newhope
Pike County
Arkansas
Death:
Apr. 20, 1946
Newhope
Pike County, Arkansas
Burial:
Langley Hall Cemetery
Langley
Pike County, Arkansas

Ed was the son of George Washington and Eliza Jane Pate Hill. He married Lucinda Jane Barentine August 17, 1902 in Howard County Arkansas. Ed was a Free Will Baptist Preacher. His name was in the Aug. 31, 1923, Minutes as pastor of Rock Springs Church

Elmer Holiman
Birth:
Sep. 3, 1926
Death:
Nov. 14, 2014
Pine Bluff,
Arkansas
Burial:
Mount Pleasant Cemetery
Plumerville
Conway County
Arkansas

Elmer Lee Holliman, 88, was a retired farmer, pastor and army veteran. He dedicated his life to sharing the gospel of Jesus Christ and leaves behind a legacy of being a man who lived what he taught. He was a member of Oak Grove Freewill Baptist Church in Lake Village.

Terrell Holland
Birth:
Apr. 21, 1929
Duncan,
Greenlee County,
Arizona
Death:
Jun. 8, 2012
Burial:
Glenwood Cemetery,
Glenwood,
Pike County, Arkansas

Rev. Terrell pastored Free Will Baptist churches in Oklahoma and Arkansas for 48 years and served at the Glenwood Free Will Baptist Church for 13 years. He was always able to bring a smile through a story, joke or encouraging word as he was concerned and loved everyone.

James Monroe Holleman
Birth:
Aug. 25, 1895,
Rose Bud, white County,
Arkansas

Death:
May 31, 1973,
RoseBud, White Cty, Arkansas
Burial:
Mount Bethel Cemetery,
Rose Bud, White County,
Arkansas

He was a Free Will Baptist minister in the New Hope Assn. james Monroe's parents were Andrew Jackson HOLLEMAN and Arminta C. (Duncan) Holleman. J. M. married Myrtle McIntire Nov. 3, 1915; she was the daughter of Charles Albert McIntire and Mary Elizabeth Boyer.
He registered for the WW I Draft June 5, 1917, with phy. description as "tall, slender, blue eyes and light brown hair, and no physical disabilities." He was on the ordination committee of this author.

David Monroe Holder
Birth:
Mar. 9, 1863
Union Point
Union County, Illinois
Death:
Mar. 1, 1934
Pocahontas
Randolph County, Arkansas
Burial:

Masonic Cemetery
Pocahontas
Randolph County, Arkansas

He came from Missouri to Arkansas about 1901-2. Living about 5 miles east of Pocahontas. He held several revivals each year and pastoring about five churches. He came from the Union Band Assn. to the Social Band.

John Robert Holt
Birth:
Nov. 27, 1868
Death:
1950
Burial:
Warm Springs Cemetery
Warm Springs
Randolph County, Arkansas

Early FWB preacher in the General Free Will Baptist Assn.

His parents were William Littleton Holt (1842 - 1926) and Nancy G. Phillips Holt (1837 - 1907). He married Carrie M. Boas Holt (1871 - 1918).

Gaylord Huckaba
Birth:
Unknown
Death:
Jan. 4, 2013
Rosie Independence County
Arkansas
Burial:
Maple Springs Cemetery,
Batesville,
Independence County, Arkansas

He was veteran and long-time Free Will Baptist pastor. His funeral message was preached by Rev. Shane King, pastor of the Blackland Chapel FWB church.

Francis Marion Hudson, Sr
Birth:
Mar. 20, 1829
Alabama
Death:
Oct. 29, 1920
Moreland
Pope County, Arkansas
Burial:
Hudson Cemetery
Moreland
Pope County, Arkansas

Francis married Mary Mary Magdelaine Yates on Jan 16, 1848 in Pope County, Arkansas, He helped organize Free Will Baptist (FWB) churches, and a J.M. Hudson's name appears in a list of moderators of the AR State Association of FWB. He also served in the Civil War, per this family history note:"F.M. Hudson Sr. enlisted as a private in the Arkansas Infantry of the Confederate Army in the War Between the States on Dec. 21, 1861 at Dardanelle, Arkansas, and served for about a year. He was in a Union Prison for war prisoners for a time."
Served as a Sergeant in Company E of the 17th Arkansas Infantry, CSA (LeMoyne's). Later served as a private in Company I of the 21st Arkansas Infantry

Earcel Huggins
Birth:
Sep. 15, 1905
Franklin County, Arkansas
Death:
Jun. 8, 1975
Crawford County, Arkansas
Burial:
Rankin Cemetery
Lone Elm
Franklin County, Arkansas,

He was a Free Will Baptist minister, listed with others in the 1957 Minutes of Zion Hope Ass'n, when it met at Walnut Street FWB Church, Ft. Smith, AR.
--from "History of Arkansas Free Will Baptists," by Rev. David A. Joslin, Editor, pub. 1998 (p.14).

Rev Oscar Clayton Hunt
Birth:
Sep. 11, 1866
Missouri
Death:
May 7, 1938
Waldron
Scott County,
Arkansas
Burial:
Lamb Cemetery
Waldron

Scott County, Arkansas

An ordained Free Will Baptist minister in AR.

Dr John Campbell Gilliland
Birth
Oct. 6, 1932
Death:
Mar. 12, 1988
Burial:
Rose Lawn Park Cemetery
Fort Smith
Sebastian County
Arkansas

Also, a minister, listed in roll from Old Mt. Zion Association of AR Free Will Baptists, showing he had died between 1980-89

Rev William Dolphis Isbell
BIRTH
2 Jan 1866
Huntsville, Madison County,
Alabama, USA
DEATH

15 Oct 1913 (aged 47)
Moreland, Pope County,
Arkansas, USA
BURIAL
Saint Joe Cemetery
Atkins, Pope County, Arkansas

Rev. Wm. D. Isbell was an ordained Free Will Baptist minister and was present at the 1900 session of the Antioch Association of FWB in Arkansas, and stated he had been ordained 8 years. The 1900 Minutes were the oldest available; therefore, he could have been in previous ones.
He was a useful minister, his name as officiant was found in obits of minister, friends and neighbors alike, in his area.

William Sherman Isbell
Birth:
May 4, 1891
Death:
Sep. 13, 1987,
Russellville,
Pope County, Arkansas
Burial:
Saint Joe Cemetery,
Atkins,
Pope County, Arkansas

Most followed his leadership due to his wisdom and firm commitment to the FWB denomination. He was an ordained minister in the Free Will Baptist Church, listed in the 1959 roll of ministers of the AR FWB State Ass'n, of which he was a member of the Antioch District, in the Pope Co. area. His name is found in these records as serving on committees, boards. In 1959, he was the AR State Ass'n statistian, the records consisting of numbers of churches, delegates, ministers, and all that pertained to that. He continuously served in that position forward for many years. He is pictured in a 1953 Ark. State Association of ministers there. (pub. Hist of ARK by Rev. David J. Joslin).

William Rufus Jobe
Birth:
Aug. 11, 1865
Death:
Jul. 24, 1938
Burial:
Shiloh Cemetery
Atkins
Pope County, Arkansas

Son of James Robert and Lizzie (Choat) Jobe. Married first to Viola Jane Norris on 17 Jul 1887, and second to Alva Duvall on 20 Oct 1895, both in Pope Co., AR. His death notice in the Northwest Arkansas Times, 25 Jul 1938: "Pea Ridge Minister Dies at Russellville: Russellville, Ark. July 25 - AP - Stricken while preaching at a revival, the Rev.

W. R. Jobe, 73, Free Will Baptist minister of the Pea Ridge Community near here, died yesterday."

Rev Clyde Franklin Johnson
Birth:
Mar. 6, 1906
Kingston
Madison County
Arkansas
Death:
Jan. 9, 1989
Fayetteville
Washington County
Arkansas
Burial:
Kingston Cemetery
Kingston
Madison County
Arkansas

Rev. Clyde Franklin Johnson, 82, of Fayetteville, Ark., at the City Hospital in Fayetteville. He was a member and former pastor of the First Free Will Baptist Church in Fayetteville. He had taught for 13 years in public schools in Madison County and had been an ordained Free Will Baptist minister for 32 years and had pastored churches in Madison and Washington counties. He was preceded in death by his wife, Mrs. Allie Virginia Lane Johnson on April 11, 1980.

Services were held at the First Free Will Baptist Church in Fayetteville, with the Rev. Dennis Artman and the Rev. Tommy Day officiating.

Joseph H. Johnson
Birth:
Apr. 1, 1854
Lawrence Co., Tennessee
Death:
Jan. 21, 1934
Washington Co., Arkansas

Burial:
Lincoln Cemetery
Lincoln
Washington County, Arkansas
Plot: row 28

He joined the Methodist Episcopal church in 1871 and received license to exhort in 1872 and to preach in 1879. He became dissatisfied with sprinkling in 1881 and joined the Free Will Baptist church at Mt. Cabo, Henderson County, Tennessee and was ordained the same year. He served as moderator of the Flat Creek Association from 1889 to 1891. He moved to Tyronza, Arkansas in 1896 and took charge of four churches—Tyronza Chapel, Dead Timber, Bullard's Chapel and Holly Grove. He was moderator in the Tyronza association in 1892-93. He was Secretary of the association in 1896 and served six years and also served as Secretary of the State Association as well as the State Evangelist two years. He pastored churches up till 1908 when he resigned pastoral work moving to Wynne in 1902 but continuing to preach.

Keith Johnson
Birth:
Jun. 4, 1934,
Alton, Oregon County,
Missouri
Death:
Jan. 11, 2010,
Conway, Faulkner County,
Arkansas
Burial:
Crestlawn Memorial Park,
Conway, Faulkner County,
Arkansas

Bro. Johnson was the pastor of First Free Will Baptist Church in Conway until just months before his death and pastored churches in Missouri and Arkansas. He managed the Christian Supply Store in Conway for 23 years.

Rev M. P. Johnson
Birth:
Oct. 21, 1855
Death:
Nov. 30, 1912
Burial:
Sharum Cemetery
Pocahontas
Randolph County, Arkansas

Early FWB preacher in the General Free Will Baptist Conference.

Rev Paul Jones
Birth
Dec. 2, 1890
Death:
Nov. 2, 1981
Burial:
Maplewood Cemetery
Harrison,Boone County
Arkansas, Plot: 2, 1A, 5

In list of Free Will Baptist ministers in the 1989 Minutes of the AR State Association of FWB. He was shown as being from the Antioch Association. Unk when he was ordained or his ministry.

David A. Joslin

Birth:
Mar. 10, 1937,
Arkansas
Death:
Sep. 10, 2011,
Conway,
Faulkner County, Arkansas
Burial:
Mount Bethel Cemetery,
Rose Bud,
White County, Arkansas

Rev. Joslin is a son of the late Rev. Joel Arthur and Clara Flossie Jones Joslin. Rev. Joslin was licensed to preach at age 19 while working as a telegrapher for the Santa Fe Railroad on an Indian reservation near Albuquerque, New Mexico. He was ordained to preach in 1957. Joslin graduated from Free Will Baptist College in Nashville, Tenn. in 1960, then attended Arkansas College in Batesville. He was Executive Director of the Arkansas Free Will Baptist State Association for 30 years after pastoring 13 years in Arkansas and Tennessee. Rev. Joslin spent 43 years of his 49-year ministry in Arkansas, pastoring six churches and helping establish two others. He served on numerous Free Will Baptist Boards including the Christian Education Board, and the General Board, the Historical Commission, and 18 years on the Executive Committee of the National Association of Free Will Baptists. Rev. Joslin founded the Ministers' Benevolent Association for Arkansas Free

Will Baptists, worked to create the guidelines for the Acts 1:8 Plan for missionary support and other denominational programs. He oversaw the publications of *"The Fifty-year Record,"* a brief historical book of the national association, and he collaborated with a group of writers in 1976 to publish *"History of Free Will Baptist State Association."* He also wrote adult Sunday School curriculum and prepared manuscripts for publication in *Contact*, the Free Will Baptist national magazine. He also edited *The Vision*, a monthly publication focusing on events and people among the 220 Arkansas Free Will Baptist churches for 30 years.

Joel Arthur Joslin

Birth:
Apr. 5, 1902,
Van Buren,
Crawford County, Arkansas
Death:
Nov. 10, 1993,
Fort Smith,
Sebastian County, Arkansas
Burial:
Gracelawn Cemetery,
Van Buren,
Crawford County, Arkansas

He was a Freewill Baptist minister, a farmer and retired employee of Missouri Pacific Railroad. He was a member of Catcher Freewill Baptist Church and had been an ordained Freewill Baptist minister since

1921. He organized the Catcher Free Will Baptist Church near Van Buren in 1930 and re-organized it in 1943. He was the father of Rev. David Joslin. He assisted in the Organization Of Several Other Free Will Baptist Churches in eastern Oklahoma and western Arkansas.

Charles Rice Kellam
Birth:
May 11, 1809
Vermont
Death:
Apr. 4, 1854
Burial:
Parks Cemetery
Charleston
Franklin County, Arkansas

He was founder of Charleston, Arkansas. Rev. Charles R. Kellam appeared in the southern part of Franklin Co. AR, via way of North Carolina, at least by 1846. In that year, he served as post-master for the area and opened the Post Office for Charleston on Aug. 10, 1846 (David Joslin, author of *"The Arkansas State Association,"*, Randall House Pub, 1976).Rev. Kellam married his wife, Susan, in N.C. and they had two children, Charles and Edward P., both bn AR, in 1850 census (by 1860, they had added Mary B.) Rev. Kellam exerted a significant influence and the commuity was named Charles Towne--later, Charleston. Rev. Kellam organized a FreeWill Baptist church in 1846, the same year he opened the post office. He remained its pastor until 1850. His work may have been brief but it was here the Arkansas District Association was organized in 1869. The church he organized was later referred to by "Goodspeed's Hist of NW AR", as a Missionary Baptist Church, but the church changed hands a number of times, and probably was a M.B. Church by the time Goodspeed's was published in 1889. After Kellam's ministry ended there in 1850, the church remained w/o a pastor until 1857. It was later reorganized, and numerous churches worshipped in the same 'meeting house,' and so confusion was not uncommon. Nevertheless, Rev. Charles Kellam did a good work and his name is found in old records and is noted here for it.He died at 45 years of age...unknown as to cause of death.

Darwin Eugene Kelton
Birth:
Mar. 13, 1937,
Roswell, Chaves County,
New Mexico
Death:
Dec. 12, 1999,
Atkins,Pope County, Arkansas
Burial:
Oakland Cemetery,
Atkins, Pope County, Arkansas

He was ordained to preach in 1974 in Fresno, California, where he chaired the Ministry Department at California Christian College. After teaching two years in Florida (1976-78),

Rev. Kelton began pastoring the First Free Will Baptist Church in Berryville, Arkansas. He served the First Free Will Baptist Church in Athens, Hatfield and Pine Hill Free Will Baptist churches until declining health required him to cease full-time pastoral duties. He served as a Minister of Music at the Union Grove church at Athens until his death. He was a gifted musician, vocally, instrumentally, and began his first radio program at age 16. He later sang with gospel quartets, directed choral groups, teach guitar lessons and guide music programs on collegiate and local church levels. He had only one eye, but his ability far exceeded the handicap as he served the Lord in many areas of the United States.

Rev James Alexander Kesner
Birth:
Mar. 19, 1853
Madison County, Arkansas
Death:
Feb. 2, 1925
Madison County, Arkansas
Burial:

Kingston Cemetery
Kingston
Madison County, Arkansas

He was a preacher and his full name was James Alexander" "James mother was Martha Hill Kesner and father was John Gatley Kesner"

Inscription:
I have fought a good fight. I have finished my course. I have kept the faith.

Ernest McKinley Kennedy
Birth:
Jan. 11, 1905
Death:
Jun. 24, 1977

Burial:
Sutton Cemetery,
Pocahontas,
Randolph County, Arkansas

He was the first State Executive Secretary in Oklahoma, begining in 1955. The office had been a part time office until the State Convention elected him. The office was in Oklahoma City.

Rev Chester U. Kinder
Birth:
Feb. 18, 1899
Death:
Sep. 16, 1964
Atkins
Pope County
Arkansas
Burial:
Saint Joe Cemetery
Atkins
Pope County
Arkansas

Rev. Kinder was an ordained minister with the Free will Baptist Church and was affiliated with the Arkansas Antioch District Association Church, at least in 1959, which records show, and probably before. Married Cassie B. Brown Aug 26 1917 in Pope County.

Dilmus Newton King

Birth:
Jan. 13, 1852
Georgia
Death:
Dec. 10, 1932
Randolph County, Arkansas
Burial:
Warm Springs Cemetery
Warm Springs
Randolph County, Arkansas

He was the son of Carter & Louisa Jane Flanigan King. He married Mary Samantha Wooldridge on 25 Jan 1872 in Warm Springs, Randolph Co, AR.

The following was taken from 1889 *Goodspeed of NE Arkansas*: Rev D.N. King, minister and farmer, Warm Springs, Ark. Although young in years, Mr King has already done much good in the world by administering to the spiritual wants of his fellowmen and by living a life of such consistency and purity as cannot fail to have its effect on the rising generation. His birth occurred in Georgia on the 13th of January 1852, and he is the son of Carter and Louisa (Flannigan) King, natives of Georgia and of Irish parentage. Carter King was a farmer and a tanner by occupation, which he followed in Georgia until 1866, when he moved to Tennessee and settled in Roan County. He there farmed on rented land until 1869, when he came to Randolph County, Ark, and settled in Warm Springs Twp, where, in 1869, he purchased eighty acres. This he proceeded to improve but one year later moved into a different neighborhood, where he died shortly afterward, in March 1871. He was a member of the Masonic fraternity, a member of the Baptist Church, and was well respected by all who knew him. He served one year during the latter part of the war in the Confederate service, and surrendered in 1865. Mr & Mrs King were the parents of eleven children, six now living: D.N., Rebecca F. (wife of F. M. Thornsberry), James M., Sarah E. (wife of H.C. Croger), Joseph J., and Mary L. (wife of James Hovis). Mrs King then married in 1873 to Rev. G. A. Barrett and by him became the mother of two children. At the age of twenty years, D.N. King was married to Miss Mary S. Wooldridge of Arkansas, and immediately afterward engaged in tilling the soil. He had very little property at the time of his marriage (1872) but he is now the owner of 160 acres, of which seventy-five acres are under a good state of cultivation and with good buildings, etc. He is one of the enterprising citizens of this section, and lays a great deal of his success in life to the exertions of his companion. He was ordained a minister in the General Free Will Baptist Church, and began preaching Gospel on the 8th of October, 1882. Since then he has performed the marriage ceremony for about nine couples and has baptized a large number of converts. Mr & Mrs King became the parents of seven children: Louisa J. born on 15th of Apriol 1873 and died on the 14th of September 1874; W.L. born on the 22d of September 1876and died on the 6th of April 1880; John C. born on the 25th of January 1879; E.E. born on the 8th of November 1881; Jasper N. born on the 10th of February 1884; Dora L. born on the 23d of August 1886 and one who died young.

Zane T. Kirkland
Birth:
unknown,
Arkansas
Death:
Feb. 2, 1992,
Little Rock
Pulaski County, Arkansas

Burial:
Strangers Home Cemetery,
Alicia,
Lawrence County, Arkansas

Pastored Free Will Baptist churches in Arkansas. He was a state leader serving on the Arkansas State Mission Board for eight years and the state Executive Board for five.
He was pastor of the Conway church at his death.

Rev Charles Cleveland Kitchens
Birth
14 Mar 1885
Death
3 Dec 1972
Burial Parks Cemetery
Nola,
Scott County, Arkansas

Rev. Charles C. Kitchens, age 87, of Gravelly, at the St Marys Hospital in Russellville. Rev. Kitchens was a Minister, a native of the Waltreak Community, a son of the late Mr. and Mrs. Charles Kitchens. Rev. Kitchens was a member of the Mulberry Freewill Baptist Church.

Survivors include his wife, Mrs. Minnie Blagg Kitchens; two sons, Jesse Kitchens of Gravelly and Ariel Kitchens of Tampa, Fla.; four daughters, Mrs. Velma Jones of Dumas, Mrs. Syble Copeland Read More of Waldron, and Mrs. Verta Seay of Georgia and Miss Etoyl Kitchens of the home; two sisters, Mrs. Decie Davison of Oklahoma and Mrs. Addie Dennis of Danville; and 21 grand-children.

Funeral services were held at the Mulberry Freewill Baptist Church with the Rev. Pat Millard officiating. Published in Yell County Record, Danville, Arkansas: 12-7-1971). He was the author of the book, *How Firm A Foundation.*

He was the grandfather of the well-known piano player Floyd Kamer.

Samuel Edward Lane
Birth:
Jul. 4, 1908

Madison County
Arkansas
Death:
Mar. 21, 1986
Rogers
Benton County
Arkansas
Burial:
Colbaugh Cemetery
Madison County
Arkansas

Listed in roll of ministers of the AR State Association of Free Will Baptists, who had died between 1980-89. He was reported from the Old Mt. Zion Dist. Unk when and where he ministered. He was Son of Joseph L and Lucy Ann Woolsey Lane and Husband of Lela Kirk Lane

Miles R. Langley
Birth:
Dec. 4, 1851
Gwinett County
Georgia
Death:
March 2, 1894
Arkansas
Burial:
Warm Springs Cemetery
Warm Springs
Randolph County, Arkansas

At the age of 17 went from Georgia to Tennessee. When twenty years old he married and moved to Randolph County, Arkansas, in 1872. Here he joined a General Free Will Baptist church and began preaching. He was ordained Oct. 7, 1876,m by Elders D. L. Poyner,

L.J. Thornbury and G. A. Barrett. He pastored four churches till a year before his death. He was one of the best pastoral preachers the denomination afforded. Among his last words were: "I am going home."

Robert Lee, Jr
Birth:
1814,
Tennessee
Death:
Apr. 22, 1887,
Madison County,Arkansas
Burial:
Lee Family Cemetery,
Aurora,Madison
County,Arkansas

An Arkansas pioneer Free Will Bapt. preacher in the late 1830's,

Herman A. Lewis
Birth:
Mar. 8, 1898,
Lebanon,
Laclede County, Missouri
Death:
Sep. 20, 1996,
Batesville,
Independence County,
Arkansas,
Burial:
Reeves Cemetery,
Melbourne,
Izard County, Arkansas

Pioneer Free Will Baptist preacher, pastor, and church planter. During his 73 years he pastored churches in Arkansas, California, & Washington. He had little education but memorized hundreds of Bible verses and quoted them extensively in his sermons. In his early ministry he pastored as many as seven churches at a time and was a widely-used revivalist he baptized hundreds of converts. He was a moderator of the Arkansas State Association during his ministry. A biography was written about him in 1974. To a grandson he wrote: "Observe with care of whom you speak, to whom you speak, and how and when and where you speak.

Rev Grady Benton Linebaugh
BIRTH
2 May 1921
Lawrence County, Arkansas
DEATH
20 Feb 2001 (aged 79)
Craighead County, Arkansas
BURIAL
Lawrence Memorial Park
Walnut Ridge, Lawrence County,
Arkansas
PLOT Section 19, New Block 3,
Between Cardinal & Robin

Grady B. was the son of Theodore Edward and Myrtle M. (Graves) LINEBAUGH. He is shown in AR 1930 & 1940 census, Randolph Co. AR in their HH with siblings. He was mar. 1) Mabel Latting Croom; 2) Juanita K Sharp.

He was a minister in the Free Will Baptist church, a member in the Social Band Association of churches which met with other associations in the AR State Ass'n of FWB in 1958, where his name was shown with other ministers. Sources: U.S., Department of Veterans Affairs BIRLS Death File,

Rev William Wallace Little
BIRTH
19 Feb 1884
Arkansas, USA
DEATH
24 Mar 1954 (aged 70)
BURIAL
Elmwood Cemetery
Morrilton, Conway County,
Arkansas
PLOT East of Mausoleum

Son of Alexander Davis Little & Ellon Nora Jane (Brigham) Little. W.W. Little married Susan Woodall 7 June 1903 in Scott County, Arkansas. William W. Little married Julia Porter 24 March 1946 in Conway County, Arkansas. Died at 70 years of age. An ordained minister in 1916 Minutes of AR State Association of FWBapt.

Rev James Silas Lovett
Birth:
Nov. 23, 1865
Death:
Mar. 30, 1957
Burial:
Cedar Grove Cemetery
Paris
Logan County, Arkansas

An ordained Free Will Baptist minister whose name appears in a list of moderators for the Arkansas State Association.

Rev George E. Lynch
Birth:
Feb. 10, 1910
Death:
Sep. 17, 1990
Burial:
Hickory Grove Cemetery
Madison County
Arkansas

Listed in Minutes of AR Free Will Baptist State Association in 1959, as an ordained minister. He was also listed as a minister again in the 1991 Minutes, from the Old Mt. Zion Association, as having died,

Curtis L. Lybarger
Birth:
Feb. 9, 1917
Death:
Jun. 29, 1993
Burial:
East Shady Grove Cemetery,
Greenbrier,
Faulkner County,
Arkansas

A Free Will Baptist minister, listed in 1959 minutes AR State Association, a minister serving in the New Hope District Association. Again, his name was in the 1998 Minutes with those who had died.

Walter B. Maddox
Birth:
Jun. 6, 1887,
Arkansas
Death:
Sep. 12, 1982,
White County,
Arkansas
Burial:

Honey Hill Cemetery,
Searcy,
White County,
Arkansas

Most of his ministry was spent in the New Hope Association in central Arkansas. Rev. W.B. Maddox was one of several ministers who org'd as the Mountain Grove Association in 1926. His name is in "Hist. of Arkansas Free Will Baptists," by Ed. David Joslin, p.53. He was on the ordaining committee of the author of this book.

Bennie P. Maness
Birth:
Aug. 18, 1898
Death:
Oct. 29, 1983
Burial:
Edgewood Memorial Park
North Little Rock
Pulaski County
Arkansas

Rev Thomas Jefferson Mantooth
Birth:
Sep. 23, 1853
Polk County
Tennessee,
Death:
Feb. 18, 1907
Burial:
Lowes Creek Cemetery
Peter Pender
Franklin County
Arkansas

Rev. T.J. Mantooth, was the son of John (b.ca 1812) and Sophia (Hall) Mantooth, of Tennessee.
He married Julia Elizabeth Rector 28 Nov. 1873, Franklin Co. AR.
He was an ordained Free Will Baptist minister serving in the Western Arkansas Ass'n, when the ARK State Ass'n of Free Will Baptists convened in 1902 in Logan Co. AR. When and where he was ordained, nor churches he pastored or assisted, is not available in the old Minutes.

--from "History of Arkansas Free Will Baptists," by Rev. David A. Joslin, Editor, pub. 1998 (pg. 58).

Dock Edgar Marchant
Birth:
Jul. 18, 1910
Death:
Jun. 13, 2000
Union Parish
Louisiana
Burial:
Woodlawn Memorial Park
Fort Smith
Sebastian County
Arkansas

Dock Marchant was a Free Will Baptist minister in Arkansas. His name is listed with other ministers in the Minutes of the Zion Hope Ass'n of FWB, in 1957, when it convened with the Walnut Street FWB Church, Ft. Smith, AR. Unknown at this date when and where he was ordained nor the churches he may have pastored.
--taken from "History of Free Will Baptists," by Rev. David A. Joslin, Editor, pub. 1998, p.14.
24 Oct 1996 Dock married Judy Alice Black Foster in Union Parish, Louisiana. His Death Certificate states that he was cremated by Kilpatrick Funeral Home in Farmerville, LA 71241.

Franklin Ray Matchett
Birth:
May 28, 1948
Athens
Pope County
Arkansas
Death:
Dec. 20, 2014
Star City, Arkansas
Burial:
Oakland Cemetery
Atkins
Pope County
Arkansas,

Franklin Ray Matchett, 66 of Star City died Saturday at his home in Star City. He was born May 28, 1948 in Atkins to the late, Delmer and Naomi Pettit Matchett. He was a retired Free Will Baptist Minister after serving the following church's over 34 years, Maple Springs, Smith Springs, Woodlawn and Yorktown. He was currently a member of Smith Springs Free Will Baptist Church in Morrilton. Frank served in the Army during the Vietnam War from 1968-1970, had Previously worked as the Parts Manager at Price Chevrolet in Morrilton, loved to garden, ride horses, write songs and poetry and sing with his family.

He was also preceded in death by his first wife of 42 years, Bonnie Sue Hubbard Matchett.

Horace Pearce McClellan
BIRTH
6 Mar 1892
Cleveland County, Arkansas, USA
DEATH
14 Apr 1981 (aged 89)
Warren, Bradley County, Arkansas, USA
BURIAL
Reaves Cemetery
New Edinburg, Cleveland County, Arkansas, USA

Son of John Patton & Margaret Eugenia McClain McClellan Minister of the gospel, and member of the Saline Association in 1958, where his name appeared in the list of ministers in that Association in AR.

Elbert McClellan
Birth:
Jun. 11, 1914,
Cleveland County, Arkansas
Death:
Apr. 6, 2010,
Pine Bluff, Jefferson County, Arkansas
Burial:
Shady Grove Cemetery, New Edinburg, Cleveland County, Arkansas

McClellan pastored Macedonia Free Will Baptist Church from 1958-60, and 1964-1966. His daughter Geraldine is married to a preacher/Bible scholar, Rev. Dr. Cecil Sanders of New Edinburg, AR, and they have a son who is a pastor, Rev. Marvin Ray Sanders of Oklahoma City, OK.

He served many congregations in southern Arkansas and member of Macedonia Free Will Baptist Church. He was a farmer and carpenter.

James Samuel McClellan
Birth:
Nov. 13, 1834
Annibelle, Abbeville County,
South Carolina
Death:
Mar. 30, 1930
Ain, Grant County, Arkansas
Burial:
Camp Creek Cemetery,
Grant County, Arkansas

Born in South Carolina, Migrating with his parents first to Georgia then to Holmes County, Mississippi by 1846. Came to Arkansas from Mississippi after July 1860 - Holmes County, Mississippi Census to Hurricane Township in what was 'old' Bradley County Arkansas, which became Dorsey in 1873 and then Cleveland County in 1885. Served in the 2nd Ark Cavalry Co. D during the Civil War attaining the rank of Corporal. Was present at the Fall of Vicksburg in 1863 by his own statement and verified in the records at Vicksburg National Battlefield Park. After he was captured at the Fall of Vicksburg with his brother David and brother in Laws, Ben Tyler and Gus Muirhead with the Vaiden Mississippi Light Artillery, he was interred for a time at the Union POW Camp, Rock Island, Illinois eventually being 'paroled' returning to Arkansas debarking at what was known as 'Red River Landing'. His enlistment papers, pension application and war records held at the Old State Capital Archives; Little Rock, Arkansas. He did receive a war pension from the State of Arkansas for his service during the Civil War Pension Record from Arkansas State Archives. He was married in 1854 to Miss Huldah Scott Mathis of Attala County, Mississippi. Patriarch of the McClellan Clan of Arkansas and the progenitor of over 1300 descendants - one Grandson was Sen. John L. McClellan, also listed on this site, elected as one of Arkansas' United States Senators for thirty-five years.

He had a long list of Free Will Baptists in southern Arkansas and FWB preachers, namely; Elbert McClellan, James Puckett, Ray Sanders, Marvin Ray Sanders, Ron Puckett, etc.

Rev David McCullough
BIRTH
2 May 1842
DEATH
16 Apr 1911 (aged 68)
Kingston,

Madison County,
Arkansas, USA
BURIAL
Drakes Creek Cemetery
Drakes Creek,
Madison County,
Arkansas, USA

The Springdale News from The Huntsville Democrat April 28, 1911.
Rev. David McCullough of near Kingston died Sunday of Brights disease with which he had been afflicted several years. The deceased was for many years a prominent minister in the Baptist Church and was widely known and esteemed throughout Madison, Boone, Carroll and Newton counties.

Robert Henry McCuin
Birth:
Nov. 23, 1940
Lake Village
Chicot County, Arkansas
Death:
Oct., 2013
Bastrop
Morehouse Parish, Louisiana
Burial:
Tate Cemetery
Hector
Pope County, Arkansas

He was the son of the late James S. and Bertha Sammons McCuin. Rev. McCuin was currently serving the Hill View Free Will Baptist Church in Bastrop, La., and pastored numerous churches across Arkansas,

Tennessee, Louisiana, Alabama, Oklahoma and Mississippi.

William Franklin McGee
Birth:
Aug. 19, 1878

Death:
Jan. 2, 1959
Russellville
Pope County,
Arkansas
Burial:
Saint Joe Cemetery
Atkins
Pope County,
Arkansas

He was an early Free Will Baptist minister and leader in the state of Arkansas. His parents were George Washington McGee and Nancy Melvina Burris. He married Alice Clemons Oct 22 1899 in Pope County.

Rev. Spartan M. McMillan's name is in a list of ministers in the 1918 Minutes of the AR State Association of Free Will Baptist, when it met at Mountain View Church.
He stated his address as Delmar, AR.
--Hist. of AR FWB, by Rev. David A. Joslin, Ed., pub. 1998.

Marriage: 1 James Henderson STRANGE b: 1829 in Spartanburg Co, SC •Married: 26 Jun 1851 in Chattooga Co, GA
Marriage: 2 Spartan M MCMILLAN b: 8 Feb 1845 in AR •Married: Bef Aug 1870 in Carroll Co, AR

Elder Spartan M. McMillan
Birth:
Feb. 8, 1845
Arkansas
Death:
Jun. 30, 1925
Carroll County
Arkansas
Burial:
Shady Grove Cemetery
Osage
Carroll County, Arkansas,

George W Million
Birth:
Sep. 25, 1877,
Randolph, Arkansas
Death:
Jan. 8, 1969,
Pocahontas,
Randolph County, Arkansas
Burial:
Masonic Cemetery,
Pocahontas,
Randolph County, Arkansas

He was a well-known preacher and author of two books on the history of Free Will Baptists. He was remembered for the use of charts while he preached. He influenced many ministers in the Social Band Association and tutored many of the early preachers that helped to form the National Association of Free Will Baptists in 1935.

R. F. Million
Birth:
Unknown
Death:
Unknown
Burial:
Sutton Cemetery
Pocahontas
Randolph County, Arkansas

Leonard L. Milligan
BIRTH
13 Jun 1911
DEATH
3 May 1996 (aged 84)
BURIAL
Lawrence Memorial Park

Walnut Ridge, Lawrence County, Arkansas, USA
PLOT   Section 15, Old Lane
Block 17-14
Between Eagle & Crane

His name was in a list of ministers from the Social Band Association of Free Will Baptists in AR in the 1958 State session for all associations.

Rev Daniel J Molloy
Birth:
Oct., 1843
Mississippi
Death:
Jul. 22, 1915
Ashley County
Arkansas
Burial:
Zion Cemetery
Hamburg
Ashley County
Arkansas

Daniel J. Molloy, became a Free Will Baptist minister as shown in old Hamburg Association of

1887 minutes, when he was elected its moderator; he gave a report of his work: which was quite active, and the monies he received that year for all his services: $30.10! When and where he was ordained is unavailable. He appeared to be active in the church until his death. Veteran: U. S. Navy

Marriage 2 Maxine Frances DOTSON b: 20 JAN 1921
Married: 9 OCT 1942
Listed in roll of Free Will Bapt. ministers, having d. from 1980-89. He was a member of the Old Mt. Zion Association when his death was reported. He was also in the 1958 roll of ministers from the same district.

Steve P Montgomery
Birth:
Madison County, Arkansas
Feb. 15, 1906
Death:
Madison County, Arkansas
Feb. 7, 1983
Burial:
Alabam Cemetery
Alabam
Madison County
Arkansas

Father: William Jones MONTGOMERY b: 17 July 1883 in Alabam, Madison Co., Arkansas-Mother: Esteller Belle HATFIELD b: 29 March 1886
Marriage 1 Jewel OWENS b: 10 July 1907 in Arkansas
Married: 1 Oct 1927 in Madison County, Arkansas.

Roy M. Moore
Birth:
Nov. 21, 1901
Death:
May 9, 1978
Burial:
Oak Grove Cemetery,
Yorktown,
Lincoln County, Arkansas

He was a popular preacher in Arkansas. It was common for him the pastored churches many miles away all the weekend should drive back to his job for Monday morning.

Rev Samuel Alexander Morgan
BIRTH
6 May 1861
Cullman County, Alabama, USA

DEATH
5 Nov 1940 (aged 79)
Naylor, Faulkner County,
Arkansas, USA
BURIAL
Pleasant Valley Cemetery
Pleasant Valley, Faulkner
County, Arkansas

Samuel had a twin brother named Zebediah. Sam was a Baptist minister. He died of Bright's Disease

Rev Jewel Franklin Morrison Jr
Birth:
Mar. 18, 1906
Crawford County, Arkansas
Death:
May 4, 1992
Van Buren
Crawford County, Arkansas
Burial:
Gracelawn Cemetery
Van Buren

Crawford County, Arkansas

He was a retired Free Will Baptist Minister and a member of the First Free Will Baptist Church of Fort Smith. He also founded and built the Oliver Springs Free Will Baptist church in 1959. He was a lifelong resident of Crawford County.
Funeral services at First Assembly of God Church Reverend Jimmy Morrison and Reverend Gilbert Pixley officiated.

Rev Frank W. Newell
BIRTH
24 Oct 1820
New Jersey, USA
DEATH
8 Mar 1908 (aged 87)
Greene County, Arkansas, USA
BURIAL
Jones Ridge Cemetery
Delaplaine, Greene County,
Arkansas

A Free Will Baptist minister, bn in Penn, (per newspaper item) but censuses show "New Jersey", lived in Kentucky where several of his children were born, then moved into Green Co. AR, about 20 years before his death, according to a newspaper item. (Greene Co. is northeastern AR). He married Isabel Fisher, bn KY. The 1900 Greene Co. census showed they were living in Jackson.

Rev A A Noggle
Birth:
Jan. 21, 1902
Georgia
Death:
Apr. 21, 1975
Arkansas
Burial:
Saint Mary's Cemetery
Rose Bud
White County
Arkansas

Rev. A. A. "Dolph" Noggle was a Free Will Baptist minister as shown in 1922 Arkansas FWB State Association Minutes, from the New Hope Ass'n #2. He was married to Nora and they had two children, Cletus D. and Flecia A. Noggle.

Rev E J O'Neal
Birth:
Dec. 9, 1864
Center Point
Howard County
Arkansas
Death:
Dec. 14, 1944
Burial:
Mount Joy Cemetery
Daisy
Pike County, Arkansas

Son of Jim & Jane O'Neal. He married Alice Golden. He was of the Baptist faith.

Rev. E.J. O'Neal (name shown Elias/Elijah in census) was an ordained Free Will Baptist minister in the early years of their work in AR. He was affiliated with the Little Missouri Association in 1902. Where and when he was ordained is unknown. He also pastored the Piney Grove Church, Pike ,Co. He was elected moderator in 1923 of the Little Missouri Association, when it met at the Mt. Joy Church, near Daisy, AR. In the 1926 Session of the AR State Ass'n of Free Will Baptists, he was one of those chosen to preach. It convened with the Glenwood FWB Church of Glenwood, in Pike Co. Sep. 30 to Oct 3, 1926. He preached a double funeral in 1927, for Charlie and Sarah Coplin, husband and wife, bur. in this cemetery.

Rev Burl Osborne
BIRTH
11 Dec 1921
DEATH
11 Oct 2001 (aged 79)
BURIAL
Gracelawn Cemetery
Van Buren, Crawford County,
Arkansas, USA

The Rev. Burl Osborne, 79, of Van Buren died Thursday, Oct. 11, 2001, in a local nursing home. He was a retired Freewill Baptist minister and cattleman and an Army veteran of World War II. Funeral Catcher Freewill Baptist Church in Van Buren.

Rev Lonnie Palmer, Jr
Birth:
Mar. 9, 1932
Pfeiffer
Independence County,
Arkansas
Death:
Aug. 23, 2015
Ada
Pontotoc County, Oklahoma
Burial:
Oaklawn Cemetery
Batesville
Independence County, Arkansas

Born to Lonnie and Minnie Williams Palmer. He came to the Allen, Oklahoma area in 2000. He married Lillian Bernice Crow on September 12, 1951. She preceded him in death in 2012. He received his degree from Free Will Bible College in Nashville, Tennessee. Rev. Palmer served as a Free Will Baptist Missionary to the Koulango, of Ivory Coast, Africa for 43 years. He formed The Association of Free Will Baptist Churches of Ivory Coast, translated The Old Testament into the Koulango language, and founded the Free Will Baptist Bible Institute of Ivory Coast.

**Missionary Bernice Crow
Palmer**
Birth:
Jan. 4, 1935
Cave City
Sharp County, Arkansas
Death:
Jan. 19, 2012
Batesville
Independence County, Arkansas
Burial:
Oaklawn Cemetery,
Batesville, Independence County
Arkansas

She served as a missionary to the Ivory Coast in Africa for 43 years. She retired from the White River Medical Center in Batesville where she worked as a registered nurse. She was a member of the Bethel Free Will Baptist Church in Allen, Oklahoma.

Rev John J Partain
Birth:
Jun. 29, 1871
Arkansas, USA

Death:
Sep. 25, 1941
Arkansas
Burial:
Harmony Cemetery
Harmony
Johnson County
Arkansas

Rev. John J. Partain, was an ordained Free Will Baptist minister in the early beginnings of the Free Will Baptist Church in AR, being named in a roll of ministers in the 1902 session convened at Paint Rock Church in Logan County. He was on a committee to help organize Sunday Schools along with two other ministers, who reported they had organized five S.S. in Mt. Zion Ass'n, (Johnson Co.) the previous year. When and where Rev. Partain was ordained is unavailable to me, but he was active in the work.
--taken from *"History of Free Will Baptists,"* by Rev. David A. Joslin, Editor, pub. 1998. [pg 57].
Rev. Partain was married to Susan A. Jacobs/Susanna Jacobs, per AR Mar records, on 27 Dec. 1891.

James Monroe Patrick
Birth:
Mar. 12, 1854
Bradley County, Arkansas
Death:
Sep. 16, 1933
Herbine
Cleveland County, Arkansas
Burial:
Prosperity Cemetery, Pansy
Cleveland County, Arkansas
Rev. Patrick, was a pioneer Free Will Baptist Minister, spent a large portion of his life in this county and was the founder of the Free Will Macedonia church in Lee Township. He was a candidate for representative from this county several times, losing twice by narrow margins. He had many friends wherever he was known. Funeral services were conducted by Rev. J. R. Hartley, lifelong friend. His spouse was Celia Jane Johnson Patrick (1859 - 1918).

Raymond Armster Patrick
Birth:
Sep. 12, 1919,
Vilonia, Faulkner County,
Arkansas
Death:
Jun. 30, 2001,
Vilonia,
Faulkner County,
Arkansas
Burial:
Cypress Valley Cemetery,
Faulkner County, Arkansas

He was a minister and pastor in central Arkansas. During his retirement years, he was a member of the Center Point Free Will Baptist Church. He was a veteran of the Navy serving during WWII.

Rev Henry Clay Pauley
Birth:
May 14, 1914
Death
Dec. 11, 1990
Piggott
Clay County
Arkansas
Burial:
Mount Zion Cemetery
Walcott
Greene County
Arkansas,

Henry Clay Pauley, 76, of Piggott, formerly of Greene County, retired minister, died Tuesday at his home. Services at Pruett's Chapel Free Will Baptist Church in Light, where he was a member.

Inscription:
CPL US Army Air Corps
World War II
May 5, 1914 - December 11, 1990

L D Payne
Birth:
Aug. 29, 1936
Death:
Oct. 27, 1997
Burial:
Oak Grove Cemetery,
Chicot County,
Arkansas

He was a popular Free Will Baptist minister serving in Arkansas pastorates. He served as Private First Class in the US Army in Korea.

Rev John Mason Perren
Birth:
Unknown
Death:
Apr., 1903
Burial:
Richwoods Cemetery
Corning Clay County. Arkansas

Obituary stated he was a minister of Free Will Church.

Bruce Erwin Phillips
Birth:
Oct. 29,1902,
Washington,
Hempstead County, Arkansas
Death:
Mar. 13, 1995,
Springdale,
Washington County, Arkansas
Burial:
Burkshed Cemetery,
Washington County, Arkansas

During the time of his ministry, he was one of the strongest leaders in northwest Arkansas among some of the oldest churches in the state.

C A Pickney
Birth:
Oct. 14, 1876
Death:
Feb. 25, 1919
Burial:
Oak Forest Cemetery
Black Rock
Lawrence County, Arkansas

Early FWB minister of the Union Band Assn. pastoring the Mt. Vernon church.
Inscription:
HUSBAND OF IDA PICKNEY

Edward Louis Pickney
Birth:
Feb., 1872
Tennessee
Death:
Nov. 24, 1958
Gentry
Benton, Arkansas
Burial:

Gentry Cemetery
Gentry
Benton County, Arkansas
Plot: Blk 11 lot 31

His home in 1900 was at Dent, Lawrence, Arkansas [Imboden, Lawrence, Arkansas] Age: 28. His father, Charles Jules Pickney (1849 - 1887) was born in France. His father married Mary Louise Yarbrough Pickney (1848 - 1924), who was born in Tennessee. Edward was married twice: Jessie Edaline McConnell Pickney (1885 - 1968) and Lucy Songer Pickney (1881 - 1919). Early FWB Minister and member of the Union Band Assn.

James H. Pierce
Birth:
Aug. 19, 1844
Death:
Jan. 24, 1922
Burial:
Thompson Cemetery
Randolph County, Arkansas

Early FWB minister pastoring the Stoney Point church and attending the Third Annual Meeting of the General Free Will Baptist at the Stoney Point church near Lima, Arkansas in 1895. Note: Civil War Veteran

Rev David W Pinkston
Birth:
Dec. 11, 1902
Arkansas
Death:
Nov. 7, 1985
Cave City
Sharp County
Arkansas
Burial:
Fairview Cemetery
Cave City
Sharp County, Arkansas

A Free Will Baptist minister, whose name is in roll of AR State Association minutes, who died between 1980-89, listing by the Districts with which they were affiliated. He was in the Social Band.

Benjamin Perry "Ben" Pixley
Birth:
Feb. 17, 1890
Death:
Nov., 1981
Fort Smith,
Sebastian County, Arkansas
Burial:
Gracelawn Cemetery,
Van Buren, Crawford County
Arkansas
The Rev. Benjamin Perry Pixley was a member of 88 Freewill Baptist Church. He was a minister for 65 years at several area Freewill Baptist churches. He was a former Mountainburg and Chester, Arkansas School board member and civic leader. He had twin sons, the Rev.

Rupert Pixley and the Rev. Gilbert Pixley of Fort Smith, Arkansas who were greatly known as Free Will Baptist ministers throughout the United States.

Gilbert J. Pixley
Birth:
Jan. 25, 1920,
Rudy,
Crawford County, Arkansas
Death:
Sep. 17, 2006,
Van Buren, Crawford County,
Arkansas
Burial:
Gracelawn Cemetery,
Van Buren,
Crawford County, Arkansas

He was a minister, pastor, and evangelist for over 60 years in Arkansas, Oklahoma, California, Texas and other states. He pastored nine churches during his career. He sang, taught music schools, and wrote songs, including a popular one, *"My*

Child, You're Home at Last," which became his epitaph. He was a Navy veteran of WW II. He and his twin brother, Rupert, were an evangelistic team for years.

He baptized the author of this book.

Rupert E. Pixley
Birth:
Jan. 25, 1920,
Arkansas
Death:
Oct. 31, 2000,
Fort Smith,
Sebastian County, Arkansas
Burial:
Gracelawn Cemetery,
Van Buren,
Crawford County, Arkansas

He was a Freewill Baptist minister for 63 years, serving the First Freewill Baptist Church in Fort Smith for 44 years before his retirement. He led this church through seven major building programs including the 700 seat auditorium that was built in 1957. In 1984 the church built a 16 thousand square-foot multipurpose building and named it the R. E. Pixley Family Center.

He was widely known as an evangelist and baptized more than 3000 converts during his ministry and the preformed over 2000 marriages. For years he had an ongoing radio ministry with a wide following. He and his twin brother, Gilbert, were known throughout the Free Will Baptists denomination as able evangelists. Many people and ministers owe their conversion to these brothers. In addition to his pastoral work, served 23 years on the Arkansas State CTS Board, a member of the State Executive Committee and served as the State Moderator. He moderated Zion Hope and Unity associations and served five years on the National Home Mission Board. At the time of his death, he was pastor of Bethlehem Free Will Baptist in Van Buren. He also was involved in the ownership of three local nursing homes.

> **The compiler of this book owes his conversion to him.**

Rev James Thelmer Ply
BIRTH
10 Jan 1921
Arkansas, USA
DEATH
11 Jan 1977 (aged 56)
Arkansas, USA
BURIAL
Oakland Cemetery
Monticello, Drew County,
Arkansas, USA

He was a minister/pastor in the southeastern part of Arkansas in the Free Will Baptist church. He was a member of the Saline Association of AR FWB and was listed as a minister in their state session in 1958.

He was the son of Floyd James Ply and Esther (Adney) PLY.

He was mar to Virginia Aileen Bogy, in AR, and they had 8 children they raised in Arkansas. James T. enlisted in the U.S. Army in Oct. 1942 in Little Rock, AR for the duration of the War II.

Dr David Scott Ponder
BIRTH
22 Nov 1976
Jonesboro,
Craighead County, Arkansas,
USA
DEATH
21 Nov 2016 (aged 39)
Walnut Ridge,
Lawrence County, Arkansas,
USA
BURIAL
Lawrence Memorial Park
Walnut Ridge,
Lawrence County
, Arkansas, USA

Dr. David Scott Ponder, 39, of Alicia passed away Walnut Ridge.He married Valerie Sturgill on December 27, 1997 in White's Creek, Tennessee.He was pastor of Arbor Grove Free Will Baptist Church.Funeral services at First Free Will Baptist Church, with Tim Campbell and Blaine Liscomb officiating.

Rev W R Porter
Birth:
Oct. 25, 1911
Death:
Oct. 3, 1982
Burial:
Manila Cemetery
Manila
Mississippi County
Arkansas

Rev Albert Alaska Powell
BIRTH
3 Jan 1877
Louisville, Jefferson County,
Kentucky, USA
DEATH
6 Oct 1949 (aged 72)
De Queen, Sevier County,
Arkansas, USA
BURIAL
Beacon Hill Cemetery
De Queen, Sevier County,
Arkansas, USA

History book by David Joslin, 1998, p. 9. Was in 1923 Association, at Mt. Joy Church, near Daisy, AR. He was from Rock Springs #1.

Jesse E Pratt
Birth:
Jan. 13, 1898
Death:
Nov. 4, 1983
Burial:
Rose Bud Cemetery,
Rose Bud,
White County, Arkansas

Most of his ministry and pastorates were all within the New Hope Quarterly Meeting. He was on the ordination committee of the author of this book.

Obadiah D "Obie" Presley
BIRTH
29 May 1881
DEATH
3 Aug 1943 (aged 62)
BURIAL
Saint Marys Cemetery
Rose Bud, White County,
Arkansas, USA

He is listed in 1926 as a Free Will Bapt. minister, in the Mountain Grove Association, in "History of Arkansas FWB, by Editor, David Joslin. His bro. Luther P. Presley was a well-known hymn/song writer of the Free Will Bapt. Persuasion,

Reuben E Pruitt, Jr
Birth:
Sep. 8, 1929
Death:
Dec. 10, 2000
Burial:
White County Memorial Gardens,
Searcy,
White County,
Arkansas

He was a popular pastor and minister in the New Hope Association in central Arkansas. He was on the ordination committee of the author of this book.

Willis L Queen

Birth:
Jan. 20, 1843
Iuka
Tishomingo County
Mississippi
Death:
Aug. 30, 1928
Logan County
Arkansas
Burial:
Carolan Cemetery
Carolan
Logan County
Arkansas

Willis L. Queen was the son of John Queen and Elizabeth Carolina "Susan" Hovis. He was first married to Vinnie Catherine Willis on September 12, 1868 in Tishomingo, Mississippi. He married his second wife, Susan Unknown, about 1885.

His name is listed in a roll of ministers in 1902 minutes of the Western Arkansas Ass'n. of Free Will Baptists, which included counties of Franklin, Logan, Scott and Sebastian.

Rev Thomas Houston Rail

Birth:
Nov. 16, 1842
Tennessee
Death
Sep. 23, 1904
Conway County
Arkansas
Burial:
Campground Cemetery
Overcup
Conway County
Arkansas

Rev. Richard Jackson Rail was married to Mary Catherine Bostian

Civil War Veteran, 117 IL Inf. Co. E; He was awarded a disability pension in 1890 for his service.
Rev. T. H. Rail, was an ordained Free Will Baptist minister in the Antioch Association of FWB, whose name appeared with those in the Arkansas State Ass'n of FWB when it met in Sept. 1902, at Paint Rock Church in Logan Co. AR. This was the fifth session of the state meeting, and the list of ministers was one of the earliest available. When and where Rev. Thomas Rail was ordained is not known at this time. He had a part in spreading the gospel in the early years of the work in Arkansas.
---taken from *"History of Arkansas Free Will Baptists"* by Rev. David A. Joslin, Editor, pub. 1998.

Rev Reece Leroy Rainwater
BIRTH
17 Jul 1891
Arkansas, USA
DEATH
14 Dec 1977 (aged 86)
Fort Smith, Sebastian County,
Arkansas, USA
BURIAL
Garden of Memories Cemetery
Charleston, Franklin County,
Arkansas, USA

J. C. Rauls
Birth:
Mar. 11, 1924,
New Edinburg,
Cleveland County, Arkansas
Death:
Mar. 5, 2010,
Monticello,
Drew County, Arkansas
Burial:
Union Cemetery,
Rye, Cleveland County, Arkansas

Bi-vocational pastor retired from
Burlington Industries and served
as a Free Will Baptist minister in
southeast Arkansas.

John Lafayette Reding
Birth:
Dec. 18, 1839
McNairy County
Tennessee
Death:
Jan. 9, 1923
Burnville
Sebastian County
Arkansas
Burial:
Mount Harmony Cemetery
Greenwood
Sebastian County
Arkansas
Plot: M-47

He was a Free Will Baptist
Minister, also a farmer. His name
is listed in the 1902 minutes of
the Western Arkansas
Association of churches. These
churches were located in
Franklin, Logan, Scott and
Sebastian Counties. Enlisted
Union Army 10 Sep 1863 at Ft
Smith, AR, age 23.into CO. F 1 AR.
INF. Son of John Thomas & Sarah
E. "Brown" Reding

Rev James M Richardson
Birth:
May 8, 1840
Tennessee
Death:
Feb. 14, 1923
Arkansas
Burial:
Plumlee Cemetery
Compton
Newton County
Arkansas

James M. Richardson, was listed in the ministers of the 1916 session of the AR State Ass'n of Free Will Baptists, when it convened at at Mountain Home, AR. He gave his age as '78', which is consistent with the DOB on his stone.

Also, noted that churches inNewton Co. (where he lived) were represented.

James Michael RICHARDSON "Enlisted:" on April 27, 1861 at Murfreesboro, Tenn. by Capt. S. N. WHITE for 12 months & "Joined for duty and enrolled:" on May 1, 1861 as a Pvt. in Capt. Stephen N. WHITE's Company, 2nd Regiment Tennessee Volunteers. & finally when the Company was "Organized and Mustered into Service of the Confederate States" on May 6, 1861 he was since listed as a Pvt., Co. A, 2nd (ROBISON's) Reg't. TN. Inf.

Rev Dewitt Columbus Ring
Birth:
Jun. 11, 1851
North Carolina
Death:
Oct. 25, 1921
Arkansas
Burial:
Macey Cemetery
Monette
Craighead County
Arkansas

In honor of the pioneer work as a minister in Arkansas.
Son of, James Ring & Parmella Quillan Ring.

Rev Andrew Jackson Rowlett
Birth:
Dec. 15, 1854
Missouri
Death:
Mar. 17, 1929
Lawrence County,

Arkansas
Burial:
Broom Cemetery
Lawrence County,
Arkansas

A.J. Rowlett was an ordained Free Will Baptist minister, his name appearing in Minutes of the 1902 AR State Ass'n of FWB, serving in the Polk Bayou Association. Where and when he was ordained is not available.
--from "History of Arkansas Free Will Baptists," by Rev. David A. Joslin, Editor, pub. 1998 [pg 58]. He was 8 when the Civil War took his father. General Order No. 11, forced the family to move down to Arkansas. He became a circuit preacher, riding all over to preach the gospel. He married Lucy in 1876 & when she died in 1918, he remarried. His second wife died in the horrible 1929 tornado that ravaged that portion of Arkansas.

Rev Albert Rozell
Birth:
Feb. 5, 1905
Death:
Jul. 16, 1988
Burial:
Gracelawn Cemetery
Van Buren
Crawford County, Arkansas,

A Free Will Baptist minister from Zion Hope #2 Association listed in names of ministers having d. from 1980-89, in David Joslin's "Hist. of AR Free Will Baptists. "His name was also in the 1950 list of ministers. Unknown when he was ordained.

Rev Othaniel Safirt
Birth
:   Apr. 8, 1910
Death:
Dec. 30, 1989

Burial:
Ballews Chapel Cemetery
Grubbs
Jackson County
Arkansas

Othaniel Safirt is listed in 1959 in AR state minutes, as a Free Will Baptist minister from Polk Bayou District Association in AR, and then later, in 1998, in a list of deceased ministers.

Rev. Robert Satterfield, 78, of Alma, Arkansas died Friday, July 9, 1993, at a Fort Smith, Arkansas hospital. He was a retired minister for Freedom Freewill Baptist Church in Alma where he had pastored 20 years. He also pastored at Oliver Springs Community Church, 81 Freewill Baptist Church, Locke Freewill Baptist Church and Pigeon Creek Freewill Baptist Church.

Funeral services were at Freedom Freewill Baptist Church in Alma, Arkansas.

Rev Robert Satterfield
Birth:
May 15, 1915
Arkansas
Death:
Jul. 9, 1993
Fort Smith
Sebastian County
Arkansas
Burial:
Mount McCurry Cemetery
Rudy
Crawford County
Arkansas

Rev Harold A Schuler
BIRTH
2 Dec 1918
Greenwood, Sebastian County,
Arkansas, USA
DEATH
27 Jul 1999 (aged 80)
Fort Smith, Sebastian County,
Arkansas, USA
BURIAL
Oak Valley Cemetery
Lavaca, Sebastian County,
Arkansas, USA

The Rev. Harold A. Schuler, 80, of Fort Smith died in a local hospital. He was a member of the First Free Will Baptist Church of Fort Smith and a Free Will Baptist Minister since 1952. He was a retiree from Harding Glass after 36 years and was a Navy veteran of World War II.

Rev Arch E Sebastion
Birth:
Aug. 19, 1902
Death:
Jul. 3, 1989
Burial:
Forest Park Cemetery
Fort Smith
Sebastian County
Arkansas

Arch E. Sabastion's name is listed in a roll of Free Will Baptist deceased ministers in the minutes of the Arkansas FWB State Association, his affiliation being with the Unity District Ass'n at the time of his death.

Rev Floyd W Scogin
Birth:
Apr. 30, 1919
Death:
Jun. 10, 2002
Burial:
Memorial Park Cemetery
Camden
Ouachita County
Arkansas

He was a Free Will Baptist minister in 1959, listed in roll of ministers in the Little Missouri River Association in Arkansas. When and where he was ordained is unavailable to me.

Benjamin Randle "Ben" Scott
Birth:
Feb. 23, 1924,
Mountain Grove,
Wright County, Missouri
Death:
May 20, 2010,
Pocahontas,
Randolph County, Arkansas
Burial:
Sutton Cemetery,
Pocahontas,
Randolph County, Arkansas

He was a Free Will Baptist minister serving as full time pastor for more than 50 years. His early pastorates were in the states of Oklahoma Missouri, and in Arkansas. He pastored First Free Will Baptist Church in Pocahontas, First Free Will Baptist Church in Jonesboro, and for twenty-four years, the First Free Will Baptist Church in North Little Rock.

In semi-retirement Bro. Scott served as interim pastor for First Free Will Baptist Church in Myrtle, Missouri; United Free Will Baptist Church in Walnut Ridge and First Free Will Baptist Church in Jonesboro. He served on numerous boards within the denomination on all levels; District Assn's, State Convention and the National Association. Bro. Scott was a member of Sutton Free Will Baptist Church in Pocahontas.

He was natural church builder and had good success at all the places where he pastored. All three of his sons are Free Will Baptist pastors. His wife Genelle was very active with and in the Woman's Auxiliary.

James Leroy Scudder
Birth:
Sep. 18, 1931
Coffman
Lawrence County
Arkansas
Death:
Jan. 22, 2014
Jonesboro
Craighead County
Arkansas
Burial:
Crossroads Cemetery
Portia
Lawrence County, Arkansas

Leroy Scudder was the son of the late Murrell and Fay Oldham Scudder. He was an ordained preacher and minister of music for many years and served at the First Freewill Baptist Church, Walnut Ridge, Arkansas, for over twenty-five years. He was employed by Scripture Press Publications for many years, a Piano Tuner and Manager of the Walnut Ridge Shepherd's Care. He was a member of the Lawrence County Ministerial Alliance. He had a brother who was a Southern Baptist minister. Leroy was a graduate of Free Will Baptist Bible College in Nashville.

He was united in marriage December 16, 1950 to Luella Bearry. Bro. David Harper and Rev. Steve Trail officiated.

Charles Freeman Seals
Birth:
Aug. 10, 1918
Kingston
Madison County, Arkansas
Death:
Oct. 25, 1990
Springdale

Washington County, Arkansas,
Burial:
Upper Campground Cemetery
Kingston, Madison County
Arkansas

Charles F. Seals, 72, died at Springdale Memorial Hospital. He was in Kingston, the son of Charlie Columbus and Ada Edna Cline Seals. He was a retired truck driver for Duncan Produce in Springdale and was a member of the Colbaugh Free Will Baptist Church. He was ordained as a Free Will Baptist minister in 1970. His name was listed in roll of "Ministers Deceased" in 1997 Minutes of the Arkansas State Association of Free Will Baptists. Services were at Sisco Chapel of Springdale with the Rev. Earl Dean Morris and the Rev. Dave Casteel officiating.

Rev Arch E. Sebastion
BIRTH
19 Aug 1902
DEATH
3 Jul 1989 (aged 86)
BURIAL
Forest Park Cemetery
Fort Smith, Sebastian County,
Arkansas, USA

Arch E. Sabastion's name is listed in a roll of Free Will Baptist deceased ministers in the minutes of the Arkansas FWB State Association, his affiliation being with the Unity District Ass'n at the time of his death.

Melvin Lee Shelton
Birth:
Mar. 13, 1922
O'Kean Randolph County
Arkansas
Death:
May 26, 2012
Jonesboro
Craighead County Arkansas
Burial:
Randolph Memorial Gardens
Pocahontas
Randolph County Arkansas

Melvin was a pastor for 64 years and had been the pastor of Northside Freewill Baptist Church in Pocahontas for the last 35 years.

Robert S Shelton
Birth:
Aug. 3, 1888,
Mountain View,
Howell County, Missouri
Death:
Oct. 31, 1954,
Old Reyno,
Randolph County, Arkansas
Burial:
Sharum Cemetery,
Pocahontas,
Randolph County, Arkansas

He was a preacher along with running his merchandise store in Okean. He was very active in the Social Band Association and a leader in the state Association.

Rev Edward W. Simpkins
BIRTH
31 Mar 1878
Barton County, Kansas, USA
DEATH
17 Jul 1963 (aged 85)
Fort Smith, Sebastian County,
Arkansas, USA
BURIAL
Forest Park Cemetery
Fort Smith, Sebastian County,
Arkansas, USA

An ordained Free Will Bapt. minister, attending and serving in local and state work.

He pastored a number of churches in Arkansas and Oklahoma and founded the First Free Will Baptist Church of Greenwood and the Cavanaugh First Free Will Baptist of Fort Smith. He also was employed by Harding Glass Co. for 31 years. He was a member of First Free Will Baptist Church for 46 years.

H. D. "Dick" Shipley
Birth:
Jul. 3, 1917,
Arkansas
Death:
Jan. 3, 1996,
Barling, Sebastian County,
Arkansas
Burial:
Gill Cemetery,
Van Buren,
Crawford County, Arkansas

Rev Isaac W. "Ike" Smith
BIRTH
16 Apr 1867
Campbell, Hunt County, Texas,
USA
DEATH
2 May 1959 (aged 92)
Idabel, McCurtain County,
Oklahoma, USA
BURIAL
Pinecrest Memorial Park
Mena, Polk County, Arkansas,

Isaac W. Smith married Mary D. Smithey May 1, 1898 Hunt County, Texas. Rev. I.W. Smith was in a roll of minister's names in the Southwestern Cooperative Association of Free Will Baptists, which met in TX in 1912; it was comprised of Texas, Missouri and Oklahoma. His long ministry and work are remembered here.

Rev Loy Smith
Birth:
Dec. 10, 1915
Death:
Feb. 4, 1967
Burial:
Mount Zion Cemetery
Jerusalem
Conway County
Arkansas,

He was a WW II U.S. Army veteran and a FWB minister..

Arvel Isaac Spears
BIRTH
29 Jul 1922
Locke, Crawford County,
Arkansas, USA
DEATH
20 Feb 2013 (aged 90)
Alma, Crawford County,
Arkansas, USA
BURIAL
Locke Community Cemetery

Fern, Franklin County, Arkansas,

He was a retired Heavy Equipment Operator, a retired minister and a U. S. Army Veteran of World War II. A minister in the Arkansas Zion Hope #2 Association of Free Will Baptists in 1958, when it met in a state-wide session. His name was in the list of ministers

Berne Ora Stahl
Birth:
Dec. 8, 1913
Arkansas
Death:
Mar. 4, 1971
Dardanelle, Yell County,
Arkansas
Burial:
Bethel Cemetery,
Kingston,Yell County, Arkansas
He had been an active minister for his last 14 years. Rev. Stahl was a native of Plainview, pastor of the Danville Free Will Baptist Church. He left many of his family active in the Lord's service. His legacy remains in them.

Oscar Avery Stapp
BIRTH
1919
DEATH
1978 (aged 58–59)
BURIAL
New Mulberry Cemetery
Mulberry, Crawford County,
Arkansas, USA

Rev Jeremiah Arnold Stark
Birth:
1848
Death:
1942
Arkansas
Burial:
Pollard Cemetery
Dover
Pope County
Arkansas

Rev. J. A. Stark was in a roll of minister's names in the 1900 Pope Co. Association meeting of the Free Will Baptists, where he stated he had been in the ministry thirteen (13) years at that time. His address was at Moreland.

--from *"History of Arkansas Free Will Baptists,"* by Rev. David A. Joslin, Editor, pub. 1998, pg. 11.

Fred B. Starnes
Birth:
Dec. 6, 1875
Death:
Oct. 20, 1909
Burial:
Jenkins Cemetery
Lawrence County, Arkansas

He was first licensed as an exhorter in the Methodist denomination but becoming dissatisfied united with the Free Will Baptists spending time in Portia and old Walnut Ridge. He was a co-worker with Elder Dave Bandy during his life-time.

Charles R Staten
Birth:
unknown
Death:
Nov. 7, 1986
Burial:
Browns Chapel Cemetery,
Paragould,
Greene County, Arkansa,
Plot: 11, row 32

His ministry was mainly in the north eastern part of the state.

Ralph Lee Staten
Birth:
Jul. 11, 1911,
O'Kean,
Randolph County, Arkansas
Death:
Oct. 6, 1997,
Knoxville,
Knox County, Tennessee
Burial:
Masonic Cemetery,
Pocahontas,
Randolph County, Arkansas

Rev Herman Lee Stubblefield
BIRTH
13 Nov 1922
Sebastian County,
Arkansas, USA
DEATH
8 Jan 2004 (aged 81)
Fort Smith,
Sebastian County, Arkansas,
USA
BURIAL
Mount Hope Cemetery
Vesta,
Franklin County,
Arkansas, USA

He was a combination itinerant pastor and public-school teacher in Northeast Arkansas in his early ministry. He later pastored in Arkansas, Alabama, Oklahoma, North Carolina and Virginia. In the early days of his ministry he was known for his debates with ministers of other denominations debating the doctrines of Free Will Baptists. He was also a writer beginning in his early ministry. He attended the 1935 organizational meeting in Nashville, Tenn. which formed the National Association of Free Will Baptists.

An ordained Free Will Baptist minister and a member in 1959 of Zion Hope #2 Association of Arkansas FWBs. Herman was a member of Mt. View Free Will Baptist Church; a 50-year life member of Charleston Lodge No. 155; past master of Charleston Lodge; past high priest R.A.M. 32nd degree life member of Western.

Rev George W. Sutton
BIRTH
15 Jan 1856
DEATH
19 Jul 1916 (aged 60)
Randolph County, Arkansas, USA
BURIAL
Sutton Cemetery
Pocahontas, Randolph County,
Arkansas, USA

Samuel Thomas Sutton
Birth:
Jul. 29, 1872
Death:
Jun. 5, 1932
Burial:
Sutton Cemetery
Pocahontas
Randolph County, Arkansas

He was the son of James F. Sutton and Ann Noblin. He married Dora B. Cannon in 1891 at Randolph Co., Arkansas and they had Ira Tom Sutton (1892 - 1974), Clarence Sutton (1899 - ___), Nellie Sutton (1907 - 1914).

Rev Lowell Lonnie Tanner
Birth:
1914
Death:
Jun. 21, 1985
Burial:
Pisgah Cemetery
Pottsville
Pope County
Arkansas

An ordained Free Will Baptist minister, who is listed in roll of deceased ministers' names from 1980-89, as recorded in the annual Minutes of the AR State Association of FWB. His name was also in a 1958 list of ministers, but unk where and when he was ordained.

Rev Andrew Franklin Taylor
Birth:
1876
Murray County, Georgia
Death:
Mar. 25, 1941
Greene County, Arkansas
Burial:
North New Hope Cemetery
Dover
Pope County, Arkansas

He was an early minister in the Free Will Baptist church,and church records show he preached in the 1913 Arkansas State Association, and he served on the temperance committee in 1918.

Elder W M Taylor
BIRTH
1 Jun 1881
Homer, Claiborne Parish,
Louisiana, USA

DEATH
27 Mar 1975 (aged 93)
Hempstead County, Arkansas,
USA
BURIAL
Rose Hill Cemetery
Hope, Hempstead County,
Arkansas, USA

Eld. Will Taylor registered for WW II Draft in Hope AR, in 1942, Stated he was b. Homer, Louisiana. His occupation: Free Will Baptist minister.
His name was in the 1916 AR Minutes of the Arkansas Dist. Ass'n, which met near Hackett, AR, and which had been organized several years earlier. Ordained ministers: ...W.M. Taylor, et al.
--p. 8, Hist of ARK FWB, by D. Joslin, pub 1998.

Elder John W. Tharp
Birth: 1882
Death: 1960
Burial:
Lawrence Memorial Park
Walnut Ridge
Lawrence County, Arkansas
Plot: Section 12,
Old Lane Block 2-11,
Between Bluejay & Bluebird

"John W. Tharp was the son of a Pennsylvanian from German descent, small of stature with a keen eye and mind.
He was ordained a Free Will Baptist minister at the Yearly Meeting of Union Band Ass'n, AR, in 1907. After his ordination he was engaged some in pastoral

supply and revival work. He united with the Social Band Association in 1910. He was pretty well posted in the scriptures, a fairly good speaker and an energetic worker."

Roy Lathan Thompson
Birth:
Jan. 16, 1938
New Edinburg,
Cleveland County, Arkansas
Death:
Dec. 7, 2002
Heber Springs,
Cleburne County, Arkansas
Burial:
Hickory Springs Cemetery,
Hermitage,
Bradley County, Arkansas

Rev Rayburn Arnold Teague
Birth:
Oct. 23, 1918
Death:
Jan. 22, 1988
Russellville
Pope County, Arkansas
Burial:
Saint Joe Cemetery
Atkins
Pope County, Arkansas

He was an ordained Free Will Baptist minister from the Antioch District Association of FWB, in 1959 church records.

Rev Lewis J Thronesberry
Birth:
Jan. 29, 1835
Bedford County, Tennessee.
Death:
Jan. 28, 1896
Burial:
Sutton Cemetery
Pocahontas
Randolph County, Arkansas

He moved with his father's family, while yet a youth, to Randolph County, Arkansas. He was one of the pioneer preachers and one of the charter members of an Independent church organized by Elder Poyner, and was ordained and did a great work. The association, as a remembrance of his labors, erected a monument at his grave. At the age of fourty was ordained to preach by the Free Will Baptist. He had a son Lewis Carlson Thronesbery (1888 - 1930).

Clarence H Tice
Birth:
Feb. 13, 1907
Marble
Madison County, Arkansas
Death:
May 1, 1985
Spring Valley
Washington County, Arkansas
Burial:
Big Sandy Church Cemetery
Purdy
Madison County, Arkansas

An ordained Free Will Bapt. minister listed in AR FWB State Association Minutes of dec'd ministers from 1980-1989. He

was affiliated with the Old Mt. Zion District Association. Unk when and where he was ordained or pastorates he held. He served during World War II. Hia Parents: John Samuel Tice (1876 - 1948) & Mary Alice Garrison Tice (1886 - 1941

Rev James Henry Treadwell
Birth: 1851
Death: 1914
Burial:
Walnut Grove Cemetery
Hector
Pope County
Arkansas

Rev John T Treadwell
BIRTH
18 Oct 1871
DEATH
12 Nov 1957 (aged 86)
BURIAL
Walker Cemetery
Weiner, Poinsett County,
Arkansas, USA

Rev Morris Lee Tucker
Birth:
Aug. 8, 1909
Rosie
Independence County
Arkansas
Death:
Mar. 14, 1989
Steelville
Crawford County
Missouri
Burial:
Maple Springs Cemetery
Batesville
Independence County
Arkansas

The Rev. Morris Lee Tucker, 79, of Steeleville, Missouri, died, at his home. He was the son of the late Robert & Bessie Young Tucker.. He married Raye Prater at Batesville on June 30, 1934. She preceded him in death on December 7, 1965. He married Hester Glenn at St. Louis, Missouri, on April 8, 1966. He was also preceded in death by his parents; a son, Don Tucker. Tucker had been a minister with the Freewill Baptist denomination since 1955. He was retired from McDonnell-Douglas Aircraft of St. Louis. At the time of his sickness & death he was attending & involved in the ministry of the 1st Baptist Church of Steeleville. Funeral services were at the Britton Brothers Funeral Home Chapel with the Rev. Dale Skiles officiating.

Remembered here as a Free Will Baptist minister, shown in list of ministers having d. from 1980-89 in "David Joslin's Hist. of AR FWB" pg 139. He was reported in the Polk Bayou FWB Dist. Association.

Wayne Tucker, Jr
Birth:
Jul. 22, 1921
Death:
Jan. 31, 1996
Burial:
Pirtle Cemetery,
Peach Orchard,
Clay County, Arkansas
His ministry was mainly in the Social Band Association in north eastern Arkansas. He served with the US Army During WWII.

Rev Elmer Turner
Birth:
Sep. 5, 1895
Branch
Franklin County, Arkansas
Death:
Apr. 10, 1987
Fort Worth
Tarrant County, Texas
Burial:
Garden of Memories Cemetery
Charleston
Franklin County, Arkansas

A Free Will Baptist minister, whose name is listed in AR State Association of FWB minutes, 1989, who had died between 1980-1989. In 1959, he was listed in same Arkansas Dist. Association on their ministers' roll.

Rev George Robert Turney
Birth:
Mar. 10, 1879
Death: 1957
Burial:
Low Gap Cemetery
Low Gap
Newton County
Arkansas

He was born at St. Joe, AR to John and Zula Eoff Turney. He was a retired minister and life resident of Boone and Searcy counties. He was 78 when he passed away at his home in Harrison, AR.

Elder John Scott Turney
Birth:
Jul. 14, 1854
Arkansas
Death:
Aug. 14, 1919
Arkansas
Burial:
Union Chapel Cemetery
Garfield
Benton County
Arkansas

Eld. John S. Turney was a pioneer Free Will Baptist minister in the old Mt. Zion Ass'n, in northeastern AR. He was listed in a roll of ordained ministers in the 1919 association minutes, stating he was 65 yrs of age. When and where he was ordained is not available.

He married Zuba Ann Eoff, and in 1900 Benton Co. AR census, stated they were m. abt 1874.

Rev Dale Wayne Underwood
BIRTH
11 Oct 1932
Vian, Sequoyah County,
Oklahoma, USA
DEATH
3 Jan 2016 (aged 83)

Checotah,
McIntosh County,
Oklahoma, USA
BURIAL
Dawson Memorial Cemetery
Milltown,
Sebastian County,
Arkansas, USA

Reverend Dale Wayne Underwood, 83-year-old Checotah resident, in Checotah, OK. He was to Cecil and Edna (Butler) Underwood in Vian, OK. Dale grew up in Vian where he attended school, graduated from Spiro High School and received his higher education from Northwestern College. He entered the United States Army on Thursday, October 13, 1949 at 17 serving for 24 years. He married the love of his life, Nancy Welch and they were united in marriage on Sunday, June 1, 1952 in Charleston, AR. He worked full time for the National Guard as a recruiter administrator. Dale taught school in Missouri for 4 years and also began preaching. He was a Free Will Baptist Minister. Dale pastored in Missouri, Arkansas and Oklahoma over 50 years. His first full time position as a Pastor was at Greenwood Free Will Baptist Church in Arkansas. He was a member of the Free Will Baptist Church in Checotah.

Rev James Buchanan Vaughan
Birth:
1857
Pope County
Arkansas
Death:
1929
Moreland
Pope County
Arkansas
Burial:
Hudson Cemetery
Moreland
Pope County
Arkansas

s/o Archibald Dodson Napier and Melissa Elizabeth (Vaughan) Napier Pinnell Brown. NOTE: They had 5 children but only 1 child was given the surname Napier for reasons unknown at this time.
James's siblings were: George Washington Vaughan b.1855; Joannah J. Napier b.1859; Telitha K. Vaughan b.1860; and Lucinda Parleen Amanda Jane Lincoln Vaughan b.1863. James B. Vaughan married Eliza M. Jones 11 March 1877 in Pope County, Arkansas. They had 4 children of whom only two lived to adulthood.

- Beckie (Carter) Williams
Joanna J. Napier was a daughter of Archibald and his wife Mary H. Vaughan, Melissa Elizabeth Vaughan's sister. The stone visible in the Napier family cemetery clearly reads M.H. as the mother. Melissa's children were all named Vaughan.

Rev Joe A Venable
Birth:
Dec. 1, 1872
Death:
Jan., 1966
Arkansas
Burial:
Saint Joe Cemetery
Atkins
Pope County, Arkansas

His name is Joseph Albert Venable, the son of Joseph Ezekiel Venable. He pastored St. Joe Free Will Baptist Church, in Adkins, AR from
1906-1908.

Robert Newton Vinson
Birth:
Mar. 3, 1845
Arkansas
Death:
Dec. 27, 1904
Pocahontas
Randolph County
Arkansas
Burial:
Thompson Cemetery
Randolph County, Arkansas

Ruben Bunyan Venable
Birth:
Jul. 12, 1877
Arkansas
Death:
Jul. 19, 1954
Atkins
Pope County,
Arkansas
Burial:
Saint Joe Cemetery
Atkins
Pope County,
Arkansas

He married Mrs. Frances Poe. 6 October 1901 in Clay Co, AR. Other spouses: Sarah F. Adair Vinson (1826 - ___), Elizabeth Ann Tyler Vinson (1857 - 1901) Minister of the Beautiful Home church and represented it at the 1895 Third Annual Meeting of the Union Band Assn. at the Stony Point Church near Lima, Arkansas.

A Free Will Baptist minister and pastor from Pope Co. AR. Listed in a 1953 photo as a minister at the Ark. State Association of FWB. His spouse: Mary Ann Atkins Venable (1876 - 1959).

Elder Hugh Warren
Birth:
Jan. 29, 1837
Indiana
Death:
Apr. 3, 1936
Johnson County
Arkansas
Burial:
Union Cemetery
Johnson County
Arkansas,

Eld. Hugh Warren, was listed in the roll of ministers of Mt. Zion Association, located principally in Johnson Co., 1904 being the earliest available minutes. When and where he was ordained is unavailable. Another, minister, William Warren, was also listed in Johnson Co. Whether related is unknown. [This info taken from *"History of Arkansas Free Will Baptists,"* by Rev. David A. Joslin, Editor, pub. 1998.]

Ray Watkins
Birth:
Jun. 22, 1905
Death:
Aug. 25, 1985
Burial:
Ballews Chapel Cemetery
Grubbs
Jackson County
Arkansas

A Free Will Bapt. minister, shown in list of dec'd ministers from 1980-89, in David Joslin's Hist. of AR FWB, pg. 139. He was reported as being from the Polk Bayou Association.

Reece G. Webb
Birth:
Jul. 10, 1900
Death:
Feb. 7, 1981
Burial:
Atkins City Cemetery
Atkins
Pope County, Arkansas

An ordained FreeWill Baptist minister in early Arkansas records. His name is listed in the roll of ministers in 1953 State Association Minutes. (see David

Joslin's *"History of Arkansas FWB."* Spouse: Ada M. Littleton Webb (1900 - 1993)*

Rev Chester F Weir
Birth:
Oct. 7, 1921
White County
Arkansas
Death:
Jul. 31, 1980
Pulaski County
Arkansas
Burial:
Weir Cemetery
Searcy
White County
Arkansas
Tec 4 US Army WWII
DS w/ Virginia

He is listed in AR Association of Free Will Baptists in a list of deceased ministers from 1980-1989. He was from the New Hope District.

Rev Bill Wheeler
Birth:
Apr. 26, 1926
Warren
Bradley County, Arkansas
Death:
Aug. 19, 2004
Little Rock

Pulaski County, Arkansas
Burial:
Willoughby Cemetery
Warren
Bradley County, Arkansas

Rev. Bill Wheeler, age 78, of Little Rock, (formerly of Warren), died at John McClellan V.A. Medical Center in Little Rock.

He was a retired Freewill Baptist minister, a mechanic and maintenance director at Camp Beaverfork, member Faith Freewill Baptist Church and a World War II Army veteran.

Funeral services were at Frazer's Chapel by Rev. Johnny Jones and Rev. Rudell Smith. Janice Sullivan was the organist and Bernadette Jones sang. Burial was in Willoughby Cemetery by Frazer's Funeral Home of Warren.

James E White
Birth:
Feb. 4, 1905
Arkansas
Death:
Jan. 10, 2000
Arkansas
Burial:
Willoughby Cemetery,
Warren,
Bradley County, Arkansas

Rev. White was the son of an ordained Free Will Baptist minister, as was his brother Stanton White. He had a long ministry in Arkansas completing over 70 years as a pastor, evangelist and church organizer. He was 94 years of age at the time of his death which was just short of his 95th birthday. He was saved at age 12 and ordained to the ministry at age 25 in 1929. His ministry was basically a bi-vocational one serving during the great depression. He labored in both south Arkansas and north Louisiana, pastoring 14 churches and organizing three.

He officiated at more than 700 funerals and finally lost the count of the number of his converts that he baptized. Rev. Ben Scott, who preached the funeral of, Rev. White, said of him, "He was a typical old-fashioned, Bible-toting, hard-hitting preacher. And was always where the action was. He was very forthright, but that the same time very tender and loving. His influence in the Saline Association was without equal. He was a moderator, served on the executive committee, examining board,

and many other positions during his time as a pastor. He was well known for his doctrinal sermons and his compassion for the lost. Jack Williams, Former *Contact* editor was saved under Brother Whites ministry, as well as many others. Brother Williams, said that the sermons of Brother White still echo in his life after more than 50 years of service.

Stanton B. White
Birth:
Mar. 14, 1913
Death:
Oct. 31, 1997
Burial:
Willoughby Cemetery,
Warren, Bradley County,
Arkansas

He was a retired machine operator for Potlatch Corp., a Freewill Baptist minister and a member of Willoughby Freewill Baptist Church at Warren. He was the son of W.P. White and a brother of J.E. White, both FWB preachers. His daughter Sue White married Bobby Aycock and they served as missionaries in Brazil.

Founders and strong leaders in building Saline Assn. in South Arkansas.

William Pleasant White
Birth:
Nov. 5, 1873
Death:
May 26, 1952
Arkansas
Burial:
Willoughby Cemetery, Warren, Bradley County, Arkansas

He was an early ordained Free Will Baptist minister, who had two sons, James E. and Stanton, who were also FWB ministers and whose influence still exists in the Saline Assn. in Southern Arkansas.

Will S. White
Birth:
Aug. 29, 1890,
Death:
Mar. 27, 1973,
Randolph County, Arkansas
Burial:
Masonic Cemetery,
Pocahontas,
Randolph County, Arkansas

He was a faithful servant coming to Christ later in life. Organizing at least four churches and ministered them until a pastor came. He was also an active schoolteacher leaving many Christian roots in his students and churches. He published a book on his life in the mid 50's that has been reprinted by FWB Publications.

Rev Isaac Jasper Whiteley
Birth:
Apr. 4, 1802
Russell County, Virginia
Death:
1889
Carroll County, Arkansas
Burial:
Liberty Cemetery
Dinsmore
Newton County, Arkansas

Son of Joseph & Sarah Ann (Stapleton) Whiteley. Married Priscilla Seehorn, March 24, 1867 Newton County, Arkansas, they later divorced. Isaac was a Tanner and a United Baptist Church Missionary.

Rev. Isaac Whiteley's name is associated with the earliest United/Free Will Baptist ministers in Arkansas. Goodspeed credits with early Arkansas church in 1837, and Isaac's bro, Samuel Whitely, also a minister, and Charles B. Whitely, were in NW AR by 1832, per family history. Isaac was in the Madison Co. 1840 census, and a land record is found for him there, in Aug. 1844.

Rev. Whiteley had 3 known wives and 10 children.

Susannah Johnston (1803-1842) married Ike in 1823 and bore him 9 children: Cynthia, Mary Elizabeth, Samuel, Joseph, Louisa, William, Nancy Adeline, Sarah Ann and Lewis W. Whiteley.

Elizabeth McCamish (1811-1867) married Ike in 1850 and bore him 1 child: James Knox Polk Whiteley.

He married Priscilla Seahorn (1805-1903) in 1867 and they divorced in 1883. They had no children.

Rev Jerrell Willingham
Birth:
Apr. 6, 1936
Beaumont
Jefferson County, Texas
Death:
Mar. 26, 2011
Little Rock
Pulaski County, Arkansas
Burial:
Shady Grove Cemetery
Atkins
Pope County, Arkansas

Rev. Jerrell Willingham, 74, of Russellville died at the Arkansas Heart Hospital.

He was born to the late William "Bill" and Versa Hamilton Willingham. He was retired from Tyson Foods and was a minister at the Egypt Free Will Paptist Church in Blue Ball. He was married to his wife, Lilla Duvall Willingham, on Sept. 24, 1955, in Russellville.Funeral services were held at Lemley Chapel with the Rev. Hank Duvall and Rev. Jackie Allen officiating.

Chester Emmit Wilson
Birth:
Jan. 9, 1897
Arkansas
Death:
Dec. 4, 1949
Pulaski Co.
Little Rock, Arkansas
Burial:
East Shady Grove Cemetery
Greenbrier
Faulkner County, Arkansas

He was an early FWB minister in Central Arkansas and pastored a number of churches in the New Hope Assn., He married a Ethel Smith in 1918 and at his passing she continued his ministry. He served in WWI Ark Pvt 158 Inf 40th Div.

Ethel E Wilson
Birth:
Dec. 14, 1901
Death:
Nov. 23, 2001
Burial:
East Shady Grove Cemetery
Greenbrier
Faulkner County
Arkansas

She was a lady minister in New Hope Assn. after assuming the ministry of her husband.

Rev Issac Jefferson Wilson
Birth:
Jun. 15, 1876
Gravelly
Yell County
Arkansas
Death:
Jun. 25, 1968
Booneville
Logan County
Arkansas
Burial:
Parks Cemetery
Charleston
Franklin County
Arkansas

Son of John Anderson Wilson and Nancy Ann Holiman. He was an ordained minister of the Freewill Baptist Church.

He obtained his nickname "one eye"due to being struck in the eye by a thorn bush limb while riding in an open wagon. The thorn pierced his eye causing him to lose vision in that eye.

IF GOD CALLED YOU TO PREACH-PREACH!!

Talmadge O.D. Winfrey
BIRTH
8 Oct 1930
Hoxie, Lawrence County,
Arkansas, USA
DEATH
12 Jan 2017 (aged 86)
Tuckerman, Jackson County,
Arkansas, USA
BURIAL
Calvin Crossing Cemetery
Alicia, Lawrence County,
Arkansas, USA

Rev. Talmadge O.D. Winfrey of Tuckerman, Arkansas, passed at his home at the age of 86. He was born the son of W.R. and Sally (Ross) Winfrey. Rev. O.D. Winfrey was a retired minister. He had been a pastor of several Free Will Baptist Churches throughout Northeast Arkansas and Southeast Missouri. He was ordained in 1950 as a minister of the Gospel, and he held true to the faith until the very end. He was a current member of the Ballew's Chapel Free Will Baptist Church in Grubbs.Rev. Winfrey also worked as a MayTag Appliance repairman in the 70's and 80's.

Rev Dewel Lee Wright
Birth:
Aug. 22, 1920
Death:
Jul. 24, 1981
Burial:
Oakland Cemetery
Atkins
Pope County
Arkansas

An ordained Free Will Bapt. minister, shown in list of dec'd ministers from 1980-89, in David Joslin's Hist. of AR FWB, pg. 139. He was from Little Missouri River Association when he died.

Rev Earnest O Wright
BIRTH
11 Sep 1897
DEATH
18 May 1970 (aged 72)
BURIAL
Saint Joe Cemetery
Atkins, Pope County, Arkansas,
USA

Rev. Earnest O WRIGHT was an ordained Free Will Baptist minister and a member of the Arkansas Antioch Association of FWB, as his stone shows, for many years.His name appears in its Minutes as a minister and clerk. Unknown when he was ordained but for so many years of service he would have been a young man.Rev. E. O. Wright's name was among the officers and ministers of the Antioch Association of Free Will Baptists in AR in its Minutes.

I bless the Christ of God,

I rest on love divine,

And with unfaltering lip and heart,

I call the Saviour mine.

His cross dispels each doubt;

I bury in his tomb

Each thought of unbelief and fear,

Each lingering shade of gloom.

www.ingramcontent.com/pod-product-compliance
Lightning Source LLC
Chambersburg PA
CBHW072210280526
45788CB00002B/960